Third Grade

Everyday
Mathematics®

Assessment Handbook

Third Grade

Everyday Mathematics®

Assessment Handbook

**The University of Chicago
School Mathematics Project**

 Wright Group

The **McGraw·Hill** Companies

UCSMP Elementary Materials Component

Max Bell, Director

Authors

Jean Bell

William M. Carroll

Acknowledgments

We gratefully acknowledge the work of the following
classroom teachers who provided input and suggestions
as we designed this handbook: Huong Banh, Fran Moore,
Jenny Waters, and Lana Winnet.

Photo Credits

Page 50, Phil Martin/Photography

Page 57, Phil Martin/Photography

Cover: Bill Burlingham/Photography

Photo Collage: Herman Adler Design

Contributors

Ellen Dairyko, Sharon Draznin, Nancy Hanvey, Laurie Leff, Denise Porter
Herb Price, Joyce Timmons, Lisa Winters

www.WrightGroup.com

Send all inquiries to:

Wright Group/McGraw-Hill

P.O. Box 812960

Chicago, IL 60681

Printed in the United States of America.

ISBN 0-07-584490-7

6 7 8 9 10 11 12 POH 10 09 08 07 06 05

The McGraw·Hill Companies

Contents

Introduction

Too often, school assessment is equated with testing and grading. While some formal assessment is necessary, it tends to provide only scattered snapshots of children rather than records of their growth and progress. The philosophy of *Everyday Mathematics*® is that real assessment should be more like a motion picture, revealing the development of the child's mathematical understanding while giving the teacher useful feedback about instructional needs. Rather than simply providing tests on isolated skills, *Everyday Mathematics* offers a variety of useful techniques and opportunities to assess children's progress on skills, concepts, and thinking processes.

Several assessment tools are built into the *Everyday Mathematics* program. Slate assessments and end-of-unit written assessments are useful in showing how well students are learning the concepts and skills covered in a unit. But these tools by themselves do not provide a balance, highlight progress, or show children's work on larger problems. The purpose of this handbook is to broaden your assessment techniques. Rather than using all of the techniques suggested here, choose a few that balance written work with observation, individual work with group work, and short answers with longer explanations.

For assessment to be valid and useful to both teachers and children, the authors believe that

- teachers need to have a variety of assessment tools and techniques from which to choose.
- children should be included in the assessment process through interviews, written work, and conferences that provide appropriate feedback. Self-assessment and reflection are skills that will develop over time if encouraged.
- assessment and instruction should be closely linked. Assessment should assist teachers in making instructional decisions concerning both individual children and the whole class.
- a good assessment plan makes instruction easier.
- the best assessment plans are those developed by teachers working collaboratively within their schools.

Home links make you think hard and some times you bring stuff in to make a museum.

A child's reflection about
Home Links

This handbook compiles classroom-tested techniques used by experienced *Everyday Mathematics* teachers. It includes suggestions for observing students, keeping anecdotal records, following student progress, and encouraging children to reflect on and communicate both what they have learned and how they feel about mathematics. Many of the assessment suggestions are aimed specifically at *Everyday Mathematics* activities, such as using Explorations to observe students or using Math Boxes to focus on a particular concept or skill.

As you read through this handbook, you may want to start with one or two activities that fit your needs and assist you in building a balanced approach to assessment. Feel free to adapt the materials to your own needs. While some teachers find Math Logs useful, others find observations and short, informal interviews more helpful.

The *Everyday Mathematics* goal is to furnish you with some ideas to make assessment and instruction more manageable, productive, and exciting, as well as offer you a more complete picture of each child's progress and instructional needs.

Name   Date   Time

Math Log A

What did you learn in mathematics this week?

446   Use as needed.

ASSESSMENT MASTER

© 2001 Everyday Learning Corporation

◆ *Math Masters*, p. 446

A Balance of Assessments

Although there is no one "right" assessment plan for all classrooms, all assessment plans should use a variety of techniques. To develop your own plan, consider four different assessment sources within the Quad shown in the figure below. The content of this handbook provides further details about these sources. The section beginning on page 39 provides examples for each unit of how to use different types of assessments in specific lessons.

Ongoing, Product, and Periodic Assessments, and Outside Tests

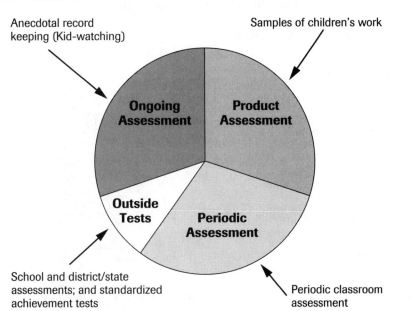

Anecdotal record keeping (Kid-watching)

Samples of children's work

Ongoing Assessment

Product Assessment

Outside Tests

Periodic Assessment

School and district/state assessments; and standardized achievement tests

Periodic classroom assessment

Ongoing Assessment includes observations of children as they are working on regular classroom activities, in groups during Explorations and games, or independently on Math Boxes. It also may include children's thinking and shared strategies as well as information you gather from classroom interactions or brief, informal, individual interviews. Records of these ongoing assessments may take the form of short written notes, more elaborate record sheets, or brief mental notes to yourself. See Ongoing Assessment, pages 13–17, for details.

Product Assessment may include samples of daily written work; group project reports; and mathematical writing, drawing, sketches, diagrams, or anything else you feel has value and reflects what you want children to learn. If you are keeping portfolios, children should help select which products to include in them. See Portfolios, pages 7–10, and Product Assessment, pages 19–23.

Periodic Assessment includes more formal assessments, such as end-of-unit assessments, quizzes, Progress Indicators, and Math Interest Inventories. Pages 25–34 offer suggestions and extensions intended to help you measure both individual and class progress using these types of assessment.

Outside Tests provide information from school, district, state, or standardized tests that might be used to evaluate the progress of a child, class, or school. See pages 35 and 36 for more information.

The types of assessment sources used within the Quad are quite flexible and depend on a number of factors, such as grade level, children's experience, time of year, and so on. For example, Kindergarten and first grade teachers, especially at the beginning of the year, probably use more of the material from the Ongoing Assessment source and less from Product and Periodic Assessment sources. In contrast, teachers in higher grades may rely more on the Product, Periodic, and Outside Assessment sources.

Flexible Quad Proportions

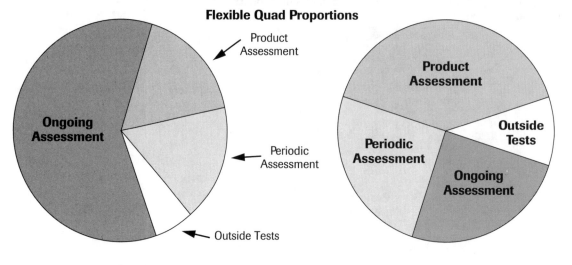

Possible First Grade Proportions

Possible Third Grade Proportions

A List of Assessment Sources attached to children's folders or portfolios or kept in your record book may help you see whether you have included information from the first three sources of the Quad as well as from other sources. Notice that the completed sample shown below includes only a few of the assessment suggestions from each source. Another teacher might choose other entries. Using multiple techniques will give you a clear picture of each child's progress and instructional needs.

Use this List of Assessment Sources master to keep track of the assessment sources that you are currently using. A blank sample is provided as *Math Masters,* page 437. The Assessment Masters, included at the back of your *Math Masters* book, are shown in reduced form on pages 80–121 of this book.

NOTE: Do not try to use all assessment sources at once. Instead, devise a manageable, balanced plan.

Your assessment plan should answer these questions:

- *How is the class performing as a whole?*
- *How are individual children performing?*
- *How can I adjust instruction to meet children's needs?*
- *How can I communicate to children, parents, and others*

List of Assessment Sources ☑

Ongoing Assessment
✓ Notes from Pattern-Block Exploration
✓ Anecdotal notes on index card
✓ Photograph of student at work in group

Product Assessment
✓ Sample Math Boxes
✓ Student project
✓ Journal page (Chosen by student)

Periodic Assessment
✓ End-of-unit assessments, Units 1–3
✓ Math Box "Quizzes"

Outside Tests

Other

Use as needed.   437

© 2001 Everyday Learning Corporation

Your Assessment Ideas

Portfolios

Using Portfolios

Portfolios are used for a number of different purposes, from keeping track of progress to helping children become more reflective about their mathematical growth. Because many schools, districts, and states are developing their own guidelines and requirements for portfolios, the *Everyday Mathematics* authors are reluctant to make specific suggestions. However, there are several reasons that the practice of keeping portfolios is positive and consistent with the philosophy of *Everyday Mathematics:*

- Portfolios emphasize progress over time, rather than results at a given moment. At any time, a child may have Beginning, Developing, or Secure understandings of various mathematical concepts. This progress can best be exhibited by a collection of products organized into portfolios or folders that contain work from different contexts and from different times in the year.

- Portfolios can involve children more directly in the assessment process. Children may write introductions and help select portfolio entries. They can select work they are especially proud of and tag each piece with an explanation of why it was chosen. The margin sample shows how a child might use self-assessment forms to tag and evaluate a piece of work. Children may need guidance in developing realistic self-assessment, which is a valuable skill that takes time to develop. Blank self-assessment forms (My Work) are provided in *Math Masters,* pages 449 and 450.

- Portfolios can be used as evidence of progress for children, their families, and their teachers for next year. You may want to establish a "Portfolio Night" for children and their parents to attend in order to allow them time to discuss and review the contents. It is very important that parents understand the goals of the various projects and assignments.

- Portfolios can illustrate children's strengths and weaknesses in particular areas of mathematics. Since a rich body of work can be contained in a portfolio, it is a good vehicle for exhibiting each child's progress. It also can be used to assess children's abilities to see connections within mathematics and to apply mathematical ideas to real-world situations.

Some teachers keep two types of portfolios: a working portfolio in which students store their recent work, and an assessment portfolio. Occasionally, a selection of work is transferred from the working portfolio to the assessment portfolio. Usually, the teacher provides some guidelines for what should be selected, allowing children to choose within these guidelines.

Many teachers recommend that the number of mathematics entries in an assessment portfolio be kept to a limited number. These entries provide a manageable but representative sample of work. New work can replace old, but some samples from throughout the year should remain.

Listed below are some ideas of representative work that might be included in a portfolio:

- Projects in progress and in completed form
- Children's solutions to challenging problems
- Written accounts of children's feelings about mathematics
- Drawings, sketches, and representations of mathematical ideas and situations
- Photographs of children interacting with manipulatives
- Photographs of children working individually and in groups
- Videos portraying children communicating mathematically

For more guidance on developing portfolio assessment, you may wish to consult one of several excellent sources listed on page 37 of this handbook. We especially recommend *Mathematics Assessment: Myths, Models, Good Questions, and Practical Suggestions,* edited by Jean Kerr Stenmark, available through the National Council of Teachers of Mathematics (NCTM). Portfolios, as well as other assessment issues, are also frequently addressed in the NCTM journal *Teaching Children Mathematics.* A video available from NCTM, *Mathematics Assessment: Alternative Approaches,* also discusses portfolios and may be helpful for teachers who are working together to develop a school-wide assessment policy.

Ideas in the *Teacher's Lesson Guide*

Portfolio Ideas Samples of children's work may be obtained from the following assignments:

Unit 1
- Continuing the Numbers Hunt (**Lesson 1.1**)
- Filling in Number Grids (**Lesson 1.2**)
- Coloring a Design (**Lesson 1.11**)
- Making a Daily Schedule of Activities (**Lesson 1.12**)
- Take a Survey (**Lesson 1.13**)
- Create Number-Grid Puzzles (**Lesson 1.13**)

Unit 2
- Comparing Data (**Lesson 2.6**)
- Making Up Addition Problems Based on a Mileage Map (**Lesson 2.7**)
- Making Up Subtraction Problems Based on a Mileage Map (**Lesson 2.8**)
- Make Up and Solve Addition and Subtraction Number Stories (**Lesson 2.10**)

Unit 3
- Simulating a Shopping Trip (**Lesson 3.7**)

Unit 4
- Solving Multiplication Stories (**Lesson 4.1**)
- Researching a "Pretend Trip" (**Lesson 4.9**)

Unit 5
- Reviewing Place-Value Concepts (**Lesson 5.1**)
- Collecting Very Large Numbers (**Lesson 5.3**)
- Collecting Very Small Numbers (**Lesson 5.7**)
- Writing about Tenths and Hundredths (**Lesson 5.9**)
- Writing Decimals with Expanded Notation (**Lesson 5.10**)

Unit 6

- Solving a Polygon Cut-Up Problem (**Lesson 6.6**)
- Symmetric (**Lesson 6.9**)
- Creating an 8-Point Design (**Lesson 6.10**)
- Create a Bulletin Board or Book of Pictures with Line Symmetry (**Lesson 6.13**)

Unit 7

- Completing My Exit Slip (**Lessons 7.4, 7.5, and 7.6**)
- Solving Problems by Estimation (**Lesson 7.7**)
- Exploring Ratio Problems (**Lesson 7.9**)

Unit 8

- Ordering Sport Balls by Diameter (**Lesson 8.5**)
- Completing My Exit Slip (**Lesson 8.7**)
- Write and Solve Fraction Number Stories (**Lesson 8.8**)

Unit 9

- Solving an Allowance Problem (**Lesson 9.2**)
- Using Count-By Patterns (**Lesson 9.4**)
- Sharing Money (**Lesson 9.7**)
- Multiplying and Dividing Multiples of 10 in the Context of Time (**Lesson 9.9**)
- Finding Number Patterns by Filling Equilateral Triangles (**Lesson 9.10**)

Unit 10

- Exploring the Volumes of Cubes (**Lesson 10.2**)
- Exploring the Meaning of Volume (**Lesson 10.3**)
- Solving Number Stories (**Lesson 10.4**)
- Connecting the Dots on a Coordinate Grid (**Lesson 10.11**)

Unit 11

- Designing, Describing, and Testing Spinners (**Lesson 11.5**)
- Math Message Follow-Up (**Lesson 11.10**)

Rubrics

One good way to keep track of each child's progress is to use a rubric. A rubric is a framework that helps you categorize progress on various aspects of a child's learning. A simple but effective rubric that many teachers use is the classification of children as Beginning, Developing, or Secure with respect to a particular skill or concept. This is illustrated below.

Sample Rubric
Beginning (B) Children cannot complete the task independently. They show little understanding of the concept or skill.
Developing (D) Children show some understanding. However, errors or misunderstandings still occur. Reminders, hints, and suggestions are needed to promote children's understanding.
Secure (S) Children can apply the skill or concept correctly and independently.

This simple rubric can be easily used with any of the sample assessment tools to keep track of the progress of individual children as well as the whole class. You may wish to use B, D, and S or another set of symbols, such as –, ✓, and +; Levels C, B, and A; or some other rubric symbols you prefer. One teacher suggests using red, yellow, and green color symbols. No matter which rubric symbols you use, you can take a quick look at a completed Class Checklist or a Class Progress Indicator to see which areas need further review or which children will benefit from additional help or challenge.

Because some children fall between Developing and Secure or may show exemplary understanding, a 3-point rubric may seem insufficient for some areas you wish to assess. This may be especially true when you are examining performance on a Project or other larger activity. A general five-level rubric follows on the next page.

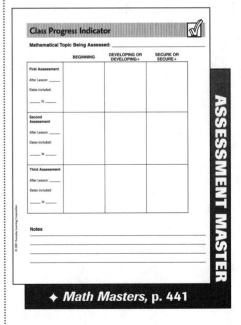

✦ Math Masters, p. 441

Sample Rubric

Beginning (B)
Children's responses may have fragments of appropriate material and may show effort to accomplish the task. However, the responses indicate little understanding of either the concepts or computational procedure involved.

Developing (D)
Children are not ready to revise their responses without conversation or more teaching. Part of the task is accomplished, but it is apparent that more understanding is needed in order for children to accomplish the entire task.

Developing+ (D+)
Responses convince you that children can revise their work in order to achieve a Secure performance with the help of feedback (in other words, teacher prompts). While understanding is good, it is not quite Secure or completely independent.

Secure (S)
Children's strategies and executions meet the content, thinking processes, and demands of the task. The responses reflect a broad range of understanding, and children can apply the understanding in different contexts.

Secure+ (S+)
A Secure+ performance is exciting. In addition to meeting the qualifications for Secure, it also merits distinction for special insights, good communication and reasoning, or other exceptional qualities.

NOTE: These rubrics are provided as an introduction to the general topic of rubrics. The most effective rubrics will be ones that you and your fellow grade-level teachers tailor to the needs of your children, as well as to the content you are teaching.

Remember, the rubrics are only a framework. When you wish to use a rubric, general indicators should be made more specific to fit the task, the time of the year, and the grade level at which the rubric is being used. Some examples of rubrics applied to specific tasks are illustrated in this book in the section on Progress Indicators/Performance Indicators beginning on page 26.

Finally, another example of a general rubric is given below. This rubric might be applied to a problem in which children are asked both to find an answer and to explain (or illustrate) their reasoning. Rubrics like these can be used to assess not only individual performance on an extended problem, but also group processes on problem-solving tasks.

Sample Rubric

Level 0
No attempts are made to solve the problem.

Level 1
Partial attempts are made. Reasoning is not explained. Problems are misunderstood, or little progress is made.

Level 2
Children arrive at solutions, and children clearly show reasoning and correct processes, but solutions are incorrect.
or:
Solutions are correct with little or no explanation given.

Level 3
Solutions are correct. Explanations are attempted but are incomplete.

Level 4
Solutions are correct. Explanations are clear and complete.

Level 5
Children offer exemplary solutions.

Ongoing Assessment

Observation of children during regular classroom interactions, as they work independently or in groups, is an important assessment technique in *Everyday Mathematics*. The following suggestions may help you manage and record these ongoing observations.

Recording Tools

Flip-Card Collection

Some teachers have found it helpful to attach index cards to a clipboard for recording observations. To do this, use one card for each child. You can use one color for the first five children, a second color for the next five children, and so on. Focus on one set of five each day, along with any other anecdotal observations from the rest of the children. Try to observe each child at least once every two weeks. Be sure to date your observations so that you can track improvements.

After a child's index card has become filled with information, remove it and file it alphabetically. Tape a new card to the clipboard to repeat the process.

The completed cards will help you keep track of children's needs and the implications for instruction. They are also useful for preparing for parent conferences.

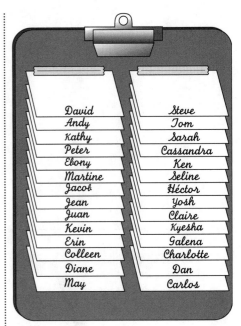

Seating Charts or Calendar Grids

Place each child's name in one of the grid cells and write observations in the cells as you circulate throughout the classroom. After reflecting on whole-class needs, cut apart the cells, date them, and file them for each child. Use them to analyze individual strengths and needs and to prepare for parent conferences.

Computer Labels

Print out children's names on sheets of large computer address labels. Write observations on the appropriate labels. As labels become filled, place them on cards or in a notebook for individual children.

> NOTE: Sequentially number the reviewed cards for each child so that you can easily see children who may have been missed (for example, you might notice that you are on Card #3 for most of the children and still on Card #1 for a few).

Observational Class Checklists

A blank checklist is provided on *Math Masters,* page 439. You may want to use it for recording ongoing observations and interactions.

So that you won't have to rewrite children's names on each checklist you use, make a copy of the blank checklist. On the copy, list the names of your children, perhaps by the groups you wish to assess at any one time. This will be your "Class Checklist" from which additional copies can be made. List the learning goals you are currently teaching and wish to assess.

The blank "Names" Master (*Math Masters,* page 440) is provided so that, if necessary, you can change the order of children's names on subsequent "Class Checklists" or on any of the grade-level checklists referred to in this handbook.

One teacher suggests attaching a blank Class Checklist to the back of a flip-card clipboard or a similar ongoing recording device and then identifying a particular concept or skill and using a rubric symbol on the checklist to indicate students' progress. (See information on Rubrics, pages 11 and 12.) Blank cells can show which children to focus on the next time you revisit the topic. The checklist indicates which children or which topics should require additional attention.

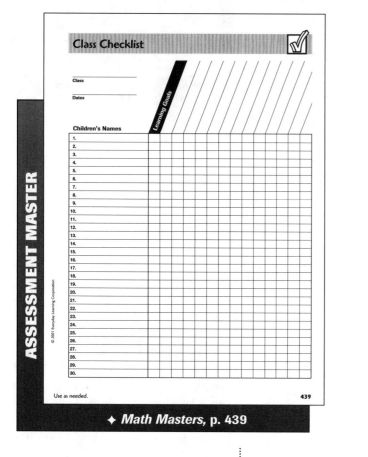

✦ *Math Masters,* p. 439

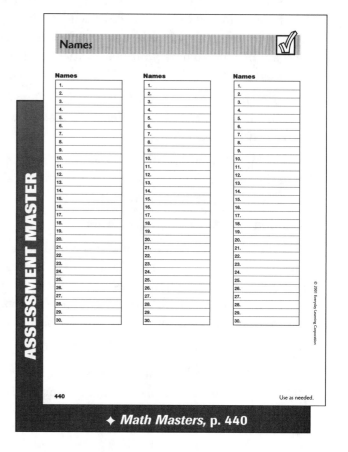

✦ *Math Masters,* p. 440

Math Box Cover-Up

Some teachers use Math Boxes to assess progress. The scenario below is from an *Everyday Mathematics* teacher.

One Teacher's Use of Math Boxes

Much of the assessment in Ms. Summers' third grade classroom is ongoing observation—short notes on progress made as children work on an activity. Generally, children are unaware that they are being assessed. For example, as children are working on a set of Math Boxes, Ms. Summers has a copy of the day's Math Boxes page attached to her clipboard and has identified particular cells that she would like to assess. These identified cells are covered with self-stick notes.

As she circulates through the classroom, Ms. Summers observes children's performance on these targeted cells. If a child is having difficulty with a particular cell, Ms. Summers may ask a probing question or two. If appropriate, the child's name is recorded on that self-stick note, sometimes with a note about the particular difficulty the child seems to be having.

Ms. Summers may also indicate the progress that she sees various children making, as well as the names of those who need extended challenges.

Later, Ms. Summers works with those children who need additional review, either individually or in a small group.

In sum, Ms. Summers uses Math Boxes to reinforce, review, and extend particular skills and concepts. If a particular concept is troublesome for the class, it will be revisited in future lessons and Math Boxes.

Ms. Summers also uses Math Boxes to communicate with parents and guardians about the mathematics being taught in the classroom and about individual children's strengths and weaknesses. Along with her observational notes, Ms. Summers finds Math Boxes to be a useful tool for assessing the progress both of her class and of individual children.

Using Recording Tools

Finding time to use the recording tools suggested in the previous section is important. Choose the one that appeals to you most and try it. If necessary, adapt it to make it more useful to you, or try another tool. Listed below are some *Everyday Mathematics* approaches and routines, with suggestions on ways to use recording tools.

Teacher-Guided Instruction

During the lesson, circulate around the room, interacting with children and observing the mathematical behavior that is taking place. Identify those children who are having difficulty, as well as those who are showing progress. Be alert to significant comments and interactions. These quick observations often tell a great deal about a child's mathematical thinking. Practice making mental notes on the spot, and follow them up with brief written notes when possible. The important thing is to find an efficient way to keep track of children's progress without getting overwhelmed with papers, lists, and notes.

Games

At the beginning of the year, when children are first becoming comfortable with the games and are playing them in small groups, move around the classroom observing the strategies that children are employing. Once children are playing the games independently, assemble a small group of those having difficulty with Math Boxes cells, computational strategies, or other related problem areas and provide help. Use the recording tools to note any valuable information regarding individual mathematical development. You can also use this time to conduct mathematical mini-interviews.

Mathematical Mini-Interviews

Observing and listening to children as they work will enable you to note progress. However, there are times when brief oral interactions with probing questions clarify and enhance observations. These brief, nonthreatening, one-on-one interactions overheard by the rest of the class or in private, as appropriate, encourage mathematical communication skills. They should, however, apply to the content at hand. For example, when children are counting as a group, you may ask some of them, "Let's see how high you can count by 3s." Or, when third graders are explaining addition strategies, you might ask, "What does the 2 in 427 mean?" or "What are the units for this number story?"

Mental Math and Reflexes

As you present the class with Mental Math and Reflexes situations, focus on a small core group of children. For example, you might start with the first five children on the clipboard or grid. You should never feel that all children need to be observed every day.

Strategy Sharing

Over time, encourage each child to share his or her strategies while working at the board or overhead projector. It is during this time that you should assume the role of "guide on the side" rather than "sage on the stage." Record which strategies the child uses. In the *Everyday Mathematics* classroom, many strategies are being utilized; recording children's strategies will help you know how to address individual strengths and needs. You will also have an opportunity to consider communication skills and processes as well as answers.

Explorations

During Explorations lessons, you can observe children participating in manipulative-based activities. As children work in small groups, you may wish to observe specific children. Another option is to establish your own workstation. As you guide children through an Exploration, note the processes, the verbalization, and the thinking that are taking place.

Slates

Periodically, record children's responses from their slate reviews. You may want to focus on one group at a time and indicate only those children with Beginning understanding. Provide follow-up instruction for them based on your notes.

Your Assessment Ideas

_____

_____

_____

_____

_____

_____

_____

_____

_____

_____

_____

_____

_____

_____

_____

_____

_____

_____

_____

_____

_____

_____

_____

_____

_____

Product Assessment

Samples of children's mathematical writings, drawing, and creations add breadth to the assessment process. In this section, the *Everyday Mathematics* authors offer suggestions and other sources for product assessment and review some of the products that are part of *Everyday Mathematics*. Some of these items can be selected and stored in a portfolio or work folder along with other assessments.

Products from *Everyday Mathematics*

Math Boxes

Math Boxes provide quick glimpses into how a child performs in several areas. As suggested in the Ongoing Assessment section of this handbook, they can also be adapted to assess topics of concern. You may find it useful to check two or three specific items that repeat throughout the year, such as Frames and Arrows or "What's My Rule?" tables.

Math Journals

Math Journals can be considered working portfolios. Children should keep the journals intact so that they can revisit, review, correct, and improve their responses at a later time. You or children might select journal pages focusing on topics of concern or number stories or pages featuring "do your own" exercises to photocopy and include in portfolios.

Math Masters

Math Masters, such as Home Links, may be collected or copied (in the case of the personal data pages) and used for product assessment. Although Home Links are less useful for assessing children because of home differences, they *can* be used to initiate discussion at parent conferences. Some teachers work on the Home Links with children in class and then send them home for discussion.

Explorations and Projects

Some of the Explorations and Projects generate 3-dimensional products that are either transitional or permanent. Displays, the use of a Polaroid camera, or brief videos can be helpful in capturing some of these products.

Additional Assessment Products

Many teachers are interested in gathering examples of children's writing and thinking in addition to those provided by *Everyday Mathematics* materials. This type of writing is usually more open-ended and provides children with opportunities to reflect, assess their understanding, and enhance their communication skills. This section offers examples of products you may want to include in your assessment plan.

Math Logs and Alternatives

Some teachers find it beneficial for children to write about mathematics regularly. A spiral notebook or a set of log sheets can be used as a Math Log. (See sample masters on *Math Masters*, pages 446–448.) Blank space is provided on the Math Log sheets so children can draw a picture or give an example of what they learned. Not only can these written reflections serve as a powerful means of checking children's understanding, but they are also a means of assessing curiosity, persistence, and self-confidence.

Remember that Math Logs are not "end products" but, instead, are an important part of the ongoing assessment process referred to on page 3. They are helpful to both you and children only if they reveal useful information and encourage the development of mathematical thinking, understanding, and written communication. Here are some suggestions on how to get children writing:

Open-Ended Questions Use open-ended questions to start children writing. Some prompts that you can use are:

• *Why is (this answer) right or wrong? Explain.*

• *What was your strategy for finding the answer?*

• *How many ways can you find an answer for this problem?*

• *How is this like something you have learned before?*

Children may use My Exit Slip sheets to record responses to open-ended questions at the close of a lesson or unit. (See *Math Masters*, page 451.)

Number Stories Occasionally ask children to write and/or draw a number story. Sometimes, you may wish to supply the numbers. For example:

• *Write a number story that uses the numbers 8 and 5.*

At other times, you may leave the instructions more open-ended:

• *Make up a number story using large numbers.*

• *Write or draw a number story that shows addition.*

Written number stories provide concrete assessment of children's understanding of operations, relationships, and numbers. For example, many children confuse addition situations with subtraction situations. Number stories often point out misconceptions.

Portfolio Writing If you are using portfolios, children can write or dictate entries for their portfolios to show what they know about numbers and mathematics. Children might dictate their ideas to you or to a classroom aide. Provide prompts like the following to encourage children to show what they already know:

• *What do you hope to learn about mathematics this year?*

• *Why is mathematics important?*

As the year continues and entries change, ask children to update their introductions and include short descriptions of the different pieces. At the end of the year, children can make a list of important things that they learned.

Concept and Strategy Writing Prior to the teaching of a unit, invite children to share what they already know about the concepts being presented. For example, before you teach a unit on multiplication, children could reflect in response to the following prompts:

• *Show me any multiplication that you can do.*

• *What is multiplication?*

• *Explain the strategy you used to solve the problem.*

• *Explain your thinking.*

Children's reflections may help you plan your instruction. At the close of each unit, ask children to respond to the same statements or questions. This allows both you and the children to compare growth in understanding of the concepts.

Later in the year, children can begin to use words, pictures, or both to explain strategies they used to solve problems. Communicating about mathematics encourages children to reflect upon their thinking and provides you with another perspective on the strategies children use. Ask a question and encourage children to write ways for solving the problem. Model this for the children.

> 6×4
> This is easy because I know that $6 \times 6 = 36$ but this is 6×4
> I just subtracted 12 because 36 has two more 6s than I need.

> ## My Math Strategies
>
> 1. 326
>   +178
>   ————
>   400
>   90
>   + 14
>   ————
>   504
>
> 2. 564
>   385 +5
>   +10
>   +100
>   64
>   ————
>   179
>
> I started with the hundreds place and added 300+100 which was 400. So then I went to the tens place and added 70+20 which was 90. So then I went over to the ones place and added 6+8 which was 14. So then I added them together and a total 400+90+14=504.
>
> First I added 5 to 385 which gave me 390+10 which gave me 400+100 to get to 500+64 that gave me 564 and I added up 5+10+100+64 and my answer was 179.

NOTE: Do not feel discouraged if children have difficulty communicating mathematically. This is a skill that takes time to develop.

Children who begin the year having nothing to say or who answer in short, incomplete sentences become much more fluent as the year progresses.

How often should you use a Math Log or other writing in your math program? This depends on you and your children. While some teachers use logs a few times per week, you may find that once a week (perhaps on Friday, reflecting on what children did that week) or at the end of the unit is sufficient.

Choose the amount of additional writing with which you and your children feel comfortable.

If you do not want to have children keep regular Math Logs, ask them to occasionally write about mathematics so that they can develop this skill. Once every unit, give children short writing assignments. Ideas can come from any of the Math Log suggestions mentioned previously in this section. These can be given as a Math Message or as part of a Math Boxes assignment. They can be short reflections written just before the end-of-unit assessment. For example:

• *The math I know best / least in this unit is* _____.

They could also be more content-oriented assignments. For example:

• *Look around the room and find two geometric shapes. Draw them and write a few sentences about them.*

Children's Reflections and Self-Assessment

Try to include children in the assessment process. The products listed below will encourage children to develop their ability to think reflectively. These products can be used as Math Messages or Home Links within the program, in Math Logs, or as alternatives to Math Logs.

Open-ended questions, such as those suggested below, provide children with opportunities to reflect on what they know and what they do not know. Invite children to reflect before, during, and/or after a lesson.

Math Masters, pages 446–451 provide alternative formats offered by experienced *Everyday Mathematics* teachers. "My Exit Slips" are suggested for responses to appropriate open-ended questions at the end of a lesson or a unit. Here are some prompts you can use:

• *My goal for tomorrow is...*
• *I learned that...*
• *I was surprised that I...*
• *I was pleased that I...*
• *I still don't understand...*
• *Because of the mathematics lesson today, I feel more confident about...*
• *The most important thing I learned in* Everyday Mathematics *today (this week) is...*
• *I think (fractions, calculators) are...*
• *(Subtraction) is easy if...*
• *The trouble with mathematics is...*
• *What I like most (or least) about* Everyday Mathematics *is...*

End-of-unit writing can help children practice self-reflection by focusing them on what they worked on during the unit.

- *In this unit, one new thing I learned is _____.*
- *One thing I still need to practice is _____.*
- *How would you explain to an absent student what we did today?*
- *What was the most difficult (easiest) part of today's lesson?*
- *Write a test problem that I might give to see if you understand today's lesson.*
- *What did you learn today that you did not know before?*
- *Tell me what you liked or disliked about today's lesson. Why?*

Sometimes you may want students to focus on how they worked in a small group:

- *What worked well in your group today?*
- *Describe what your job was in your group today.*
- *What could you have done to help your group work better?*
- *What do you like or dislike about working in a group?*

This kind of writing may give teachers some ideas about children's attitudes toward mathematics and about which experiences have been the most beneficial. Responses will vary, depending on the writing and reflective experiences of children.

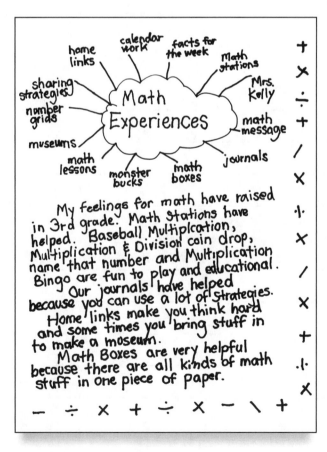

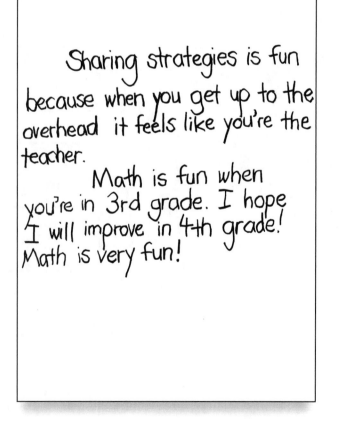

Your Assessment Ideas

_____

_____

_____

_____

_____

_____

_____

_____

_____

_____

_____

_____

_____

_____

_____

_____

_____

_____

_____

_____

_____

_____

_____

Your Assessment Ideas

Periodic Assessment

Periodic assessment activities are those that are done at fairly consistent times or intervals over the school year. We will briefly review periodic assessment sources that are currently part of *Everyday Mathematics* and then discuss additional sources that experienced teachers use.

Sources from *Everyday Mathematics*

Unit Reviews and Assessments

Each unit of your *Teacher's Lesson Guide* ends with a review and assessment lesson that lists the learning goals for that unit. The goals list is followed by a cumulative review that includes suggestions for oral and slate assessments as well as a list of the written assessment items from the Checking Progress Assessment Masters for the unit. Each of these written assessment items is matched to one or more of the learning goals.

This cumulative oral, slate, and written review provides an opportunity for you to check children's progress on concepts and skills that were introduced or further developed in the unit.

Some additional reminders:

- Use rubrics to record children's progress toward each learning goal you assess. Rubrics are introduced on pages 11 and 12 of this book, and examples of how to use them are provided on pages 28–31 and in the Assessment Overviews section beginning on page 39.

- Only concepts and skills that are the focus of several activities within any given unit are suggested for assessment at the end of a unit. However, feel free to add concepts and skills that you particularly want to assess or skills from previous units that you wish to reassess.

- Since many of the end-of-unit reviews and assessments tend to focus on skills, you may want to add more conceptual and open-ended questions as suggested in the Product Assessment section of this book, beginning on page 19.

> NOTE: If needed, generate your own reviews and quizzes for periodic review and assessment.
>
> Please give us feedback on your review and assessment ideas; this information may be beneficial to other teachers.

Math Boxes and Other *Math Journal* Pages

You can use rubrics to periodically assess Math Boxes and other *Math Journal* pages as independent reviews. By recording appropriate rubric symbols on a Class Progress Indicator (see page 27) or a Class Checklist, you can ascertain which children may need additional experience and perhaps pair or group them with children who offer Secure responses.

Midyear and End-of-Year Assessments

The Midyear and End-of-Year Assessment Masters (*Math Masters,* pages 392–403) provide additional assessment opportunities that you may wish to use as part of your balanced assessment plan. Minis of these masters, with answers, are shown on pages 91–97 of this book. These tests cover important concepts and skills presented in *Third Grade Everyday Mathematics,* but they are not designed to be used as "pre-tests" and they should not be your primary assessment tools. Use them along with the ongoing, product, and periodic assessments that are found within the lessons and at the end of each unit.

Additional Sources

Progress Indicators/Performance Indicators

Class Progress Indicators, also known as Performance Indicators, are another assessment tool that some teachers have found useful in assessing and tracking children's progress on selected mathematical topics. For example, early in third grade, you would expect most students to be Beginning or Developing when writing multiplication number stories. However, by spring, some children will be Secure, and the rest should be Developing. Progress of the whole class, as well as individual children, can be assessed periodically, and appropriate instruction planned accordingly.

A Class Progress Indicator form provides space to record children's performance on any mathematical topic you choose to assess two or three times during the year.

The first assessment opportunity, which usually occurs after children have some exposure to and experience with a topic, provides a baseline for your children's performance early in the year. By recording the second and third assessments on the same form, you can track the progress of each child as well as the whole class throughout the school year. A third grade teacher's sample Class Progress Indicator is shown on page 27. A blank form of this master is provided in *Math Masters,* page 441.

Record the names of children under the columns that most accurately indicate their levels: Beginning, Developing, or Secure (or whichever rubric symbols you want to use). If you wish, use a plus symbol (+) to indicate children who are between the given levels. As you conduct your assessments, keep this question in mind: *What do I need to do instructionally to promote progress?* Space is provided at the bottom of the form for any notes you may wish to make.

Class Progress Indicator

Mathematical Topic Being Assessed: _Multiplication Number Stories_

	BEGINNING	DEVELOPING OR DEVELOPING+		SECURE OR SECURE+	
First Assessment After Lesson: _4.2_ Dates included: _Nov. 22_ to _Nov. 30_	John Sarah Jason Patrick Juan Keiko Matthew Herb Tiffany	Toya Donna George Michael Justin Roderick Kenya Bobby Jenny		Paul Sharon Keisha	
Second Assessment After Lesson: _7.9_ Dates included: _Jan. 23_ to _Jan. 27_	Matthew Jason Herb Tiffany John Sarah Sam	Patrick Juan+ Maria LaTisha+ Toya Donna George Michael Justin	Roderick Kenya Jenny+ Camille Keiko Bobby	Paul+ Sharon Keisha Gregory Kate Molly	
Third Assessment After Lesson: _9.5_ Dates included: _Apr. 18_ to _Apr. 21_	Matthew Tiffany Jason	Herb John Sarah+ Toya+ Donna Roderick Bobby+ Camille+ Patrick+	Sam	Juan Maria LaTisha George Michael Justin Kenya+ Jenny Keiko	Paul+ Sharon+ Keisha Gregory Kate Molly

Notes

1st Assessment: Revisit Multiplication Number Stories several times a week!

Goal: Move Beginning Kids into Developing

2nd Assessment: Worried about kids. Do I need to set up Exploration station to give them more practice time?

Use as needed. 441

You may adapt the general rubric (Beginning, Developing, Developing+, Secure, Secure+) to your particular class level. On the pages that follow, we offer examples for two mathematical topics and accompanying rubrics.

For each of these topics, suggested assessment times are provided along with specific rubrics. Use the rubric provided or feel free to adapt one to your own class. A blank rubric form is provided on page 443 of _Math Masters_. Use the Class Progress Indicator to assess and record student understanding of other topics (for example, Frames and Arrows, Numeration, and so on). However, do not try more than two or three the first time through.

The teachers who prepared the following examples reported that creating these specific topic rubrics was not an easy task. Collaborating with colleagues proved helpful. The process takes time, but it becomes easier and is well worth the effort.

NOTE: Ideally, a group of grade-level teachers should go through the same assessments using a B, D, S rubric. Comparing the results and discussing differences, they should arrive at a consensus and record the results to form an appropriate rubric for the topic being assessed.

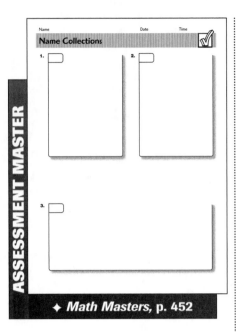

◆ Math Masters, p. 452

Example 1: Name-Collection Boxes

Name-collection boxes were introduced in First Grade *Everyday Mathematics* as a means of providing children with experience of the powerful mathematical concept that any number can be expressed in many equivalent ways. In the beginning, children primarily used addition and subtraction facts for equivalencies of relatively small numbers. By third grade, children will be expected to begin to include some multiplication and division representations (pictures, arrays) and perhaps numerical expressions for the equivalencies of larger numbers.

Time Frame: Since name-collection boxes have been used in first grade, assessments with Class Progress Indicators can begin early in the year, sometime after the review in Lesson 1.6, using *Math Journal 1,* page 8; or Home Link 1.6; or Grade 3 Activity Master A (*Math Masters,* page 452) for the first assessment.

Follow-up assessments can be made anytime you feel Beginning and Developing children have had more experience with equivalencies. As a minimum, an assessment can be made at least once and possibly twice again during the year.

Sample Name-Collection Box Rubric for Third Grade

Sample Rubric
Beginning (B) Children use primarily one operation for the name-collection box, often with one single-digit number as a part of an expression. Addition and subtraction fact extensions are sometimes used.

Developing (D)
Children use a wider variety of operations to express equivalencies, including more complicated addition and subtraction statements. There are also some simple multiplication and division expressions.

$$39 + 11 = 50$$

卌 卌 卌
卌 卌 卌
卌 卌 卌
卌

$$10 \times 5$$

fifty   half of 100
$32 + 18$ $100 \div 2$

X X XX X X X X X X
X X X X X X X X X X
XX X X X X X X X X
X X XX X X X X X XX
XXXX

Secure (S)
Children show strong evidence of understanding equivalence. Multiple operations may be used for one equivalent expression, such as 10 + (2 • 3), along with more complicated single-operation equivalencies, including multiplication and division. Equivalent names may include fractions, some being expressed as decimals.

Fifty

卌 卌 卌 卌 卌
卌 卌 卌 卌 卌

$\frac{1}{8}$ of 400

$(5 \times 6) + 20 = 50$

$\frac{1}{20}$ of 1,000

$5 \times 10 = 50$

$500 \div 10 = 50$

$5,000 \div 100 = 50$

$25 \times 2 = 50$

$27 + 23 = 50$

LL
xx + xxx
Ⓠ Ⓠ

Example 2: Algorithm Invention

Everyday Mathematics believes that children should be encouraged to "invent" procedures and share their thinking when solving problems with whole-number multidigit numbers. As they gain experience, many children refine these strategies for use on a more permanent basis. In other words, they develop their own algorithms. Some children will need more help over time in developing procedures that they understand and use regularly.

Time Frame: This framework has been a part of *Everyday Mathematics* since first grade. The initial assessment using the Class Progress Indicator can be a part of Lesson 2.7, in which procedures for adding multidigit numbers are reviewed.

Initial assessments for the other operations can be made on separate Class Progress Indicators throughout the year as they are reviewed or introduced. Follow-up for all operations can be made at least once more and perhaps two more times during the year.

Sample Addition Algorithm Rubric

Sample Rubric

Beginning (B)
Children's responses may have fragments of appropriate procedures and show efforts toward solutions. However, it is clear that children are unsure of place-value concepts and really do not understand, or have not developed, procedures that have meaning.

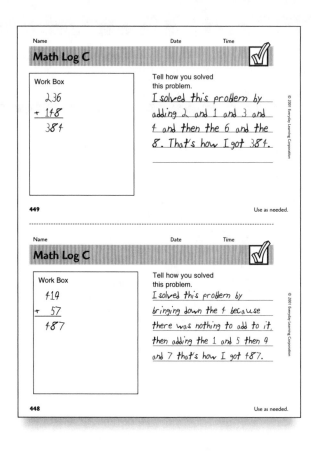

Developing (D)

Part of the computational procedure may be correct. But it is clear that more help and experience are required for complete development of accurate, fairly consistent addition procedures that children use with confidence.

Math Log C

Name   Date   Time

Work Box

```
  670
+ 240
  960
```

Tell how you solved this problem.

I take the 670 and add 200 and that wold eaKult 870 but then I add the 90

450   Use as needed.

Math Log C

Name   Date   Time

Work Box

```
  180
+  56
  236
```

Tell how you solved this problem.

I take the 56 but I made 56 into 58 and I adde the 178 and it eaKind 236

448   Use as needed.

NOTE: Remember, the more experience you have with the range of children's responses, the easier it will be to determine or assign rubrics.

Secure (S)

Children employ a correct computational procedure fairly consistently in most multidigit addition situations. There is clear evidence that children understand the notion of place value, as well as how the procedures themselves work.

Math Log C

Name   Date   Time

Work Box

```
  236
+ 148
  384
```

Tell how you solved this problem.

I did 236 + 150 then subtracted 2 and that = 384

451   Use as needed.

Math Log C

Name   Date   Time

Work Box

```
  419
+  57
  476
```

Tell how you solved this problem.

I did 57 + 420 and I subtracted 1 and = 476

448   Use as needed.

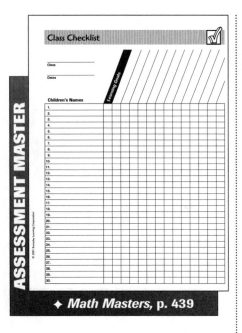

✦ Math Masters, p. 439

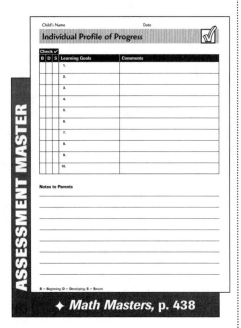

✦ Math Masters, p. 438

NOTE: Class Checklists and
Individual Profiles of Progress are
only two parts of your assessment
program. Observations of children
as they work, as well as samples of
their work, are necessary to provide
a full picture of children's
understandings and abilities.

Class Checklists and Individual Profiles of Progress

Class Checklists and Individual Profiles of Progress are provided for
each unit as well as for each quarter. These checklist and profile
masters list the learning goals identified for the end-of-unit oral
and written assessments. They are found at the back of your *Math
Masters* book and are reproduced in the Assessment Masters section
of this book on pages 97–113.

First, use the Class Checklists to gather and record information.
Then, transfer selected information to the Individual Profiles of
Progress sheet for each child's portfolio or for use during parent
conferences.

The information recorded on the checklists can be obtained from
end-of-unit oral and written assessments. In fact, you may want to
bypass the Class Checklists and record this information from these
assessments directly onto the Individual Profiles of Progress.

Blank profile and checklist masters can be found on *Math Masters,*
pages 438 and 439. You may wish to record information from other
sources, such as journal review pages, Math Boxes, Math Messages,
and Math Logs.

Information obtained from teacher-directed small groups and
organized during Explorations, game time, or any other time is
also a good resource to be recorded on the Class Checklists or
directly on Individual Profiles of Progress. As mentioned in the
Ongoing Assessment section of this book, information can be
obtained from observations, questions, and other sources during
regular instructional interactions as well.

When you use Class Checklists and Individual Profiles of Progress,
consider using a rubric-recording method, such as Beginning,
Developing, or Secure, to indicate progress. After children have had
more experience and time with various concepts and skills, repeat
needed assessment activities to assess progress further.

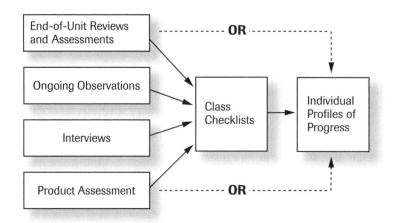

As an additional resource, you may choose to use *Math Masters*, page 440 which provides additional blank "Names" columns if you need to change the order for listing children's names on your master Class Checklist.

✦ *Math Masters*, p. 440

ASSESSMENT MASTER

Individual Mathematical Interviews

Periodically interview children individually over the course of the year. These interviews should be kept short (10 to 15 minutes long at most). Getting to each child is not something that can be done very often, but even a couple of times a year should suffice.

Main objectives of interviews

• To show children that you are concerned about them as individuals
• To get to know children better
• To find out how children feel about mathematics and what they know about mathematics

When to hold interviews

Interviews can be conducted while the rest of the class is playing games or during fairly independent Explorations. Teachers have also suggested that, if feasible, you can make "appointments" to have lunch with children individually or with two or three children at a time. Other appointments might be scheduled before class begins, during recess, or after school.

Suggestions for starting interviews

The focus of these interviews should reflect the information you are interested in discovering from individual children. Sample questions you may want to ask are:

• *How do you feel about mathematics?*
• *What have you enjoyed most about mathematics this year? What has been the easiest part of mathematics for you?*
• *What has been the hardest part of mathematics for you?*
• *How can we work together to help you feel more comfortable with these difficult parts of mathematics?*
• *How do you feel about working with partners and in small groups for some mathematics activities?*
• *How do you feel about Home Links? About Math Boxes?*

Children's responses might be taped or recorded on an individual interview sheet.

Math Interest Inventories

At the beginning of the year, you may want children to complete an inventory to assess their mathematical attitudes. This inventory might be repeated later in the year to see if their attitudes have changed. Two grade-level samples (About My Math Class) are given in *Math Masters,* pages 444 and 445. Inventories can be included in children's portfolios and discussed during individual interviews or parent conferences. For younger children, discussion of portfolios might be best done in individual or small-group interviews.

Parent Reflections

Parents can also be included in the assessment process. Prior to conferences, you can send parents a Parent Reflections page. A sample is given below. A blank Parent Reflections form is provided in *Math Masters,* page 442. The prompts are designed to focus parents' concerns prior to conferences.

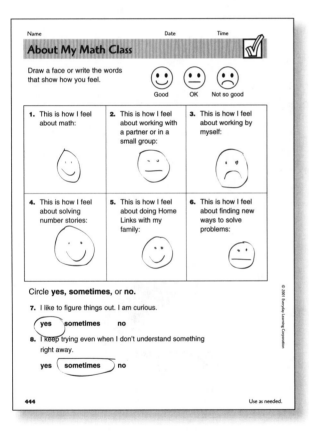

Child's Name *Linda G.*   Date *1/2/2000*

Parent Reflections

Use some of the following questions (or your own) and tell us how you see your child progressing in mathematics:

Do you see evidence of your child using mathematics at home?

What do you think are your child's strengths and challenges in mathematics?

Does your child demonstrate responsibility for completing Home Links?

What thoughts do you have about your child's progress in mathematics?

Linda surprises me with her grasp of math concepts and by the fact that she actually thinks about mathematical problems in her everyday life.
Sometimes she'll tell me how she figured out a math problem. At first it may seem like a long, roundabout process, but then I realize she's just using the tools she has and inventing her own formulas.
She takes full responsibility for doing her Home Links—the pages are out of her bag before her coat is off after school.

442   Use as needed.

Outside Tests

Many teachers are responsible for outside tests or assessments that are mandated by their schools, districts, or states. These tests vary widely, from traditional standardized tests with multiple-choice responses to more performance-based assessments. Because of the attention that is sometimes given to outside tests and assessments, many teachers worry whether *Everyday Mathematics* adequately prepares students, especially for the traditional standardized test formats.

Reports from teachers and school administrators indicate that *Everyday Mathematics* children generally do about as well on the computation sections of standardized tests—and much better on the concepts and problem-solving sections as students in traditional programs. Our research supports these anecdotal reports. However, traditional standardized tests do not assess the depth and breadth of the mathematical knowledge that should be attained in a well-implemented *Everyday Mathematics* classroom.

Many testing companies, as well as several states, districts, and schools, have recently developed performance assessments or open-ended tests. These tests indicate results similar to those from traditional tests—class and individual norms (percentile rankings)—but they also attempt to test problem-solving and communication skills on larger tasks. Some of these assessments provide rubric scores along with normed data.

Some standardized tests, along with many state tests, now allow the use of calculators on problem-solving sections because many students have access to them during instruction. Here are some further suggestions for handling outside tests:

- Rather than taking class time to "teach to the test," you may want to rely on Math Boxes and a systematic review of completed Math Boxes problems to help prepare children for the format of an outside test. It is our experience that it is the unfamiliar format and the test-taking conditions that disturb children, especially younger children, the most when taking outside tests.

NOTE: There is a blank Math Boxes master at the back of the Teaching Masters section of your *Math Masters* book (page 199). You might want to use it to fill in your own Math Boxes problems.

- If your district test is based on traditional goals, work toward having it rewritten to match the National Council of Teachers of Mathematics *Assessment Standards* and the *Everyday Mathematics* curriculum.
- Encourage or consider the use of one of the newer performance-based tests in place of the traditional multiple-choice standardized tests. As much as possible, outside tests should reflect the instructional practices of the classroom.

Your Assessment Ideas

_____

_____

_____

_____

_____

_____

_____

_____

_____

_____

_____

_____

_____

_____

_____

_____

_____

_____

_____

_____

_____

_____

Recommended Reading

Black, Paul, and Dylan Wiliam. "Assessment and Classroom Learning." *Assessment in Education* (March, 1998): 7–74.

———. "Inside the Black Box: Raising Standards Through Classroom Assessment." *Phi Delta Kappan* 80, no. 2 (October, 1998): 139–149.

Bryant, Brian R., and Teddy Maddox. "Using Alternative Assessment Techniques to Plan and Evaluate Mathematics." *LD Forum* 21, no. 2 (winter, 1996): 24–33.

Eisner, Elliot W. "The Uses and Limits of Performance Assessment." *Phi Delta Kappan* 80, no. 9 (May, 1999): 658–661.

Kuhn, Gerald. *Mathematics Assessment: What Works in the Classroom*. San Francisco: Jossey-Bass Publishers, 1994.

National Council of Teachers of Mathematics (NCTM). *Curriculum and Evaluation Standards for School Mathematics*. Reston, Va.: NCTM, 1989.

———. *Assessment Standards for School Mathematics*. Reston, Va.: NCTM, 1995.

———. *Principles and Standards for School Mathematics: Discussion Draft*. Prepared by the Standards 2000 Writing Group. Reston, Va.: NCTM, 1998.

National Research Council, Mathematical Sciences Education Board. *Measuring What Counts: A Conceptual Guide for Mathematics Assessment*. Washington, D.C.: National Academy Press, 1993.

Pearson, Bethyl, and Cathy Berghoff. "London Bridge Is Not Falling Down: It's Supporting Alternative Assessment." *TESOL* Journal 5, no. 4 (summer, 1996): 28–31.

Shepard, Lorrie A. "Using Assessment to Improve Learning." *Educational Leadership* 52, no. 5 (February, 1995): 38–43.

Stenmark, Jean Kerr, ed. *Mathematics Assessment: Myths, Models, Good Questions, and Practical Suggestions*. Reston, Va.: National Council of Teachers of Mathematics, 1991.

Stiggens, Richard J. *Student-Centered Classroom Assessment*. Englewood Cliffs, N.J.: Prentice-Hall, 1997.

Webb, N. L., and A. F. Coxford, eds. *Assessment in the Mathematics Classroom: 1993 Yearbook*. Reston, Va.: National Council of Teachers of Mathematics, 1993.

Your Assessment Ideas

Assessment Overviews

This section offers examples for each unit of how to use different types of assessments in specific lessons. For each unit, you will find examples of three major types of assessment opportunities: Ongoing Assessment, Product Assessment, and Periodic Assessment. Keep in mind, however, that these are not distinct categories; they frequently overlap. For example, some Periodic Assessments may also serve as Product Assessments that you or the child may choose to keep in the child's portfolio.

Contents		Page

Unit 1
Assessment Overview

There are many pathways to a balanced assessment plan. As you teach Unit 1, start to become familiar with some of the approaches to assessment. The next few pages provide examples of the three major types of assessment suggested in this program: Ongoing Assessment, Product Assessment, and Periodic Assessment. This assessment overview offers examples of ways to assess children on what they learn in Unit 1. Do not try to use all of the examples, but begin with a few that meet your needs.

Ongoing Assessment Opportunities

Ongoing assessment opportunities are opportunities to observe children during regular interactions, as they work independently and in groups. You can conduct ongoing assessment during teacher-guided instruction, Math Boxes sessions, mathematical mini-interviews, games, Mental Math and Reflexes sessions, strategy sharing, and slate work. The chart below provides a summary of ongoing assessment opportunities in Unit 1, as they relate to specific Unit 1 learning goals.

1d **Developing/Secure Goal** Tell and show times to the nearest minute. (Lesson 1.4)	Lesson 1.4, p. 32
1e **Developing/Secure Goal** Calculate the values of combinations of bills and coins and write the totals using dollars-and-cents notation. (Lessons 1.9 and 1.10)	Lesson 1.9, pp. 56 and 57
1f **Secure Goal** Find equivalent names for numbers. (Lesson 1.6)	Lesson 1.6, p. 42
1g **Secure Goal** Know addition facts. (Lessons 1.3, 1.4, and 1.6)	Lesson 1.6, p. 42

Product Assessment Opportunities

Math Journals, Math Boxes, activity sheets, masters, Math Logs, and the results of Explorations and Projects all provide product assessment opportunities. Here is an example of how you might use a rubric to assess children's ability to create number-grid puzzles.

Lesson 1.13, p. 80

ALTERNATIVE ASSESSMENT **Create Number-Grid Puzzles**

Circulate as children create number-grid puzzles for their partners to solve. Lesson 1.2 provides instructions for solving and creating number-grid puzzles. For this activity, ask children to write in more than one number in each puzzle in order to assess their ability to solve number-grid patterns. The sample rubric below can help you evaluate children's work.

Portfolio Ideas

Sample Rubric
Beginning (B) The child attempts to create a number-grid puzzle but experiences difficulty as a result of a lack of understanding of the patterns on the number grid. (When you move one column to the right, increase by 1; when you move one column to the left, decrease by 1; when you move 1 row up, decrease by 10; when you move 1 row down, increase by 10.) Therefore, the child may write only one number in each puzzle.
Developing (D) The child is able to create number-grid puzzles by providing at least two numbers in each puzzle. The child is able to work with any of the numbers 1–110.
Secure (S) The child is able to create number-grid puzzles without assistance from the teacher. The child uses numbers that go beyond the Class Number Grid. For example, he or she might write 3- or 4-digit numbers.

Periodic Assessment Opportunities

Here is a summary of the periodic assessment opportunities that are provided in Unit 1. Refer to Lesson 1.13 for details.

Oral and Slate Assessment

In Lesson 1.13, you will find oral and slate assessment problems on pages 77 and 78.

Written Assessment

In Lesson 1.13, you will find written assessment problems on page 79 (*Math Masters,* pages 369 and 370).

See the chart on the next page to find oral, slate, and written assessment problems that address specific learning goals.

1a	**Developing/Secure Goal** Identify and use number patterns to solve problems. (Lessons 1.2 and 1.11)	Written Assessment, Problems 1–3, 13, and 14
1b	**Secure Goal** Count by 10s and 100s. (Lesson 1.2)	Oral Assessment, Problems 1–4 Slate Assessment, Problem 4 Written Assessment, Problems 7, 8, and 13
1c	**Developing/Secure Goal** Apply place-value concepts in 4-digit numbers. (Lessons 1.2 and 1.3)	Slate Assessment, Problems 1, 2, and 4 Written Assessment, Problems 8 and 9
1d	**Developing/Secure Goal** Tell and show times to the nearest minute. (Lesson 1.4)	Slate Assessment, Problem 6 Written Assessment, Problems 10–12
1e	**Developing/Secure Goal** Calculate the values of combinations of bills and coins and write the totals using dollars-and-cents notation. (Lessons 1.9 and 1.10)	Oral Assessment, Problem 5 Written Assessment, Problems 4 and 5
1f	**Secure Goal** Find equivalent names for numbers. (Lesson 1.6)	Slate Assessment, Problem 5 Written Assessment, Problems 6 and 15
1g	**Secure Goal** Know addition facts. (Lessons 1.3, 1.4, and 1.6)	Written Assessment, Problem 15

Alternative Assessment

In Lesson 1.13, you will find alternative assessment options on pages 79 and 80.

✦ Play *Name That Number*

Assess children's skill at finding equivalent names for numbers, as well as their knowledge of addition and subtraction facts, by using this game from Lesson 1.6. Use Flip Cards or a Class Checklist as you circulate. Alternatively, you might have children record each number sentence on a half-sheet of paper for a written assessment. Consider the following questions:

• Can the child find more than one name for a number?

• Does the child use addition and subtraction to find names for a number?

✦ Play *Beat the Calculator*

Assess children's knowledge of addition facts by using this game from Lesson 1.8. You might ask children to record the facts on half-sheets of paper for which they did not beat the calculator. Collect the papers, and keep the following questions in mind:

• Do children know most addition facts?

• Which facts do they need to practice most?

David
Andy
Kathy
Peter
Ebony
Martine
Jacob
Jean
Juan
Kevin
Erin
Colleen
Diane
May

Steve
Tom
Sarah
Cassandra
Ken
Seline
Héctor
Yosh
Claire
Kyesha
Galena
Charlotte
Dan
Carlos

✦ Create Number-Grid Puzzles

As children create number-grid puzzles for their partners to solve, assess their ability to identify and use number-grid patterns. Collect children's work and use the sample rubric on page 41 in the Product Assessment Opportunities section of this book as you assess their abilities. Alternatively, circulate and keep the following questions in mind:

• Can the child find patterns on a number grid?

• Can the child use the patterns to make puzzles?

✦ Take a Survey

Assess children's ability to organize and analyze data by using this activity that requires them to develop and conduct a survey. Lesson 1.5 provides background information for this activity. Use Flip Cards or a Class Checklist as you circulate. Keep such questions as the following in mind:

• Can the child write a question that can be easily answered?

• Can the child record his or her results accurately with a tally chart?

• Is the child able to display the results of his or her survey in a bar graph?

• Does the child's summary of what he or she has learned reflect his or her actual survey results?

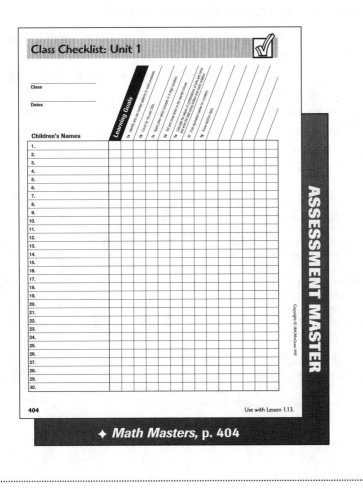

✦ *Math Masters*, p. 404

Unit 2
Assessment Overview

If you tried some of the assessment approaches that were suggested in the Unit 1 Assessment Overview, you are probably beginning to appreciate how the goal charts in this section can help you plan your assessment strategies. For example, at this point children are expected to be at a Secure level for the basic addition and subtraction facts (see Goal 2d in the chart below), and the chart alerts you to the fact that an ongoing assessment opportunity related to that goal is provided in Lesson 2.1 on page 93 of your *Teacher's Lesson Guide.* In similar fashion, you can use the chart on page 46 to find oral and written assessment opportunities related to this same goal.

Ongoing Assessment Opportunities

Ongoing assessment opportunities are opportunities to observe children during regular interactions, as they work independently and in groups. You can conduct ongoing assessment during teacher-guided instruction, Math Boxes sessions, mathematical mini-interviews, games, Mental Math and Reflexes sessions, strategy sharing, and slate work. The chart below provides a summary of ongoing assessment opportunities in Unit 2, as they relate to specific Unit 2 learning goals.

2b	**Developing/Secure Goal** Use basic facts to solve fact extensions. (Lessons 2.2, 2.3, and 2.5)	Lesson 2.3, p. 107 Lesson 2.5, p. 119
2c	**Developing/Secure Goal** Complete "What's My Rule?" tables. (Lesson 2.3)	Lesson 2.3, p. 107
2d	**Secure Goal** Know addition and subtraction facts. (Lesson 2.1)	Lesson 2.1, p. 93
2e	**Secure Goal** Complete fact and number families. (Lesson 2.1)	Lesson 2.1, p. 95
2f	**Developing/Secure Goal** Solve addition and subtraction multidigit number stories. (Lessons 2.4–2.6 and 2.9)	Lesson 2.5, p. 116 Lesson 2.6, p. 126
2g	**Developing/Secure Goal** Add multidigit numbers. (Lessons 2.7 and 2.9)	Lesson 2.7, p. 132

Product Assessment Opportunities

Math Journals, Math Boxes, activity sheets, masters, Math Logs, and the results of Explorations and Projects all provide product assessment opportunities. Here is an example of how you might use a rubric to assess children's ability to solve addition and subtraction number stories.

Lesson 2.10, p. 150

ALTERNATIVE ASSESSMENT **Make Up and Solve Addition and Subtraction Number Stories**

Children write and solve parts-and-total number stories involving addition and subtraction. Lesson 1.2 provides instructions for this activity. Circulate and assess children's progress as they create their stories. The sample rubric below can help you evaluate children's work.

Portfolio Ideas

Sample Rubric

Beginning (B)
The child is able to write a parts-and-total number story for addition with little teacher assistance. The child might require more assistance, however, to write a subtraction parts-and-total story. The unit box is complete, but the child might use single-digit numbers when the expectation is that the child will use at least 2-digit numbers. The child makes an attempt to draw the parts-and-total diagrams, but they are incomplete. The number model might be missing or incorrect.

Developing (D)
The child is able to write at least one addition and one subtraction number story involving 2-digit (and in some cases 3-digit) numbers. The parts-and-total diagrams are filled in correctly, except for occasional computational errors.

Secure (S)
The child is able to create addition and subtraction number stories using 2-, 3-, or 4-digit numbers. He or she completes parts-and-total diagrams for each story with correct number models.

Periodic Assessment Opportunities

Here is a summary of the periodic assessment opportunities that are provided in Unit 2. Refer to Lesson 2.10 for details.

Oral and Slate Assessment

In Lesson 2.10, you will find oral and slate assessment problems on pages 147 and 148.

Written Assessment

In Lesson 2.10, you will find written assessment problems on page 149 (*Math Masters,* pages 371–373).

See the chart on the next page to find oral, slate, and written assessment problems that address specific learning goals.

2a	**Developing Goal** Estimate answers to multidigit addition and subtraction problems. (Lessons 2.2, 2.7, and 2.8)	Written Assessment, Problems 11–16
2b	**Developing/Secure Goal** Use basic facts to solve fact extensions. (Lesson 2.2)	Slate Assessment, Problems 1–3 Written Assessment, Problems 2–6
2c	**Developing/Secure Goal** Complete "What's My Rule?" tables. (Lesson 2.3)	Written Assessment, Problems 3–6
2d	**Secure Goal** Know addition and subtraction facts. (Lesson 2.1)	Oral Assessment, Problems 1 and 2 Written Assessment, Problem 1
2e	**Secure Goal** Complete fact and number families. (Lesson 2.1)	Written Assessment, Problems 1 and 2
2f	**Developing/Secure Goal** Solve addition and subtraction multidigit number stories. (Lessons 2.4–2.6 and 2.9)	Written Assessment, Problems 7–10
2g	**Developing/Secure Goal** Add multidigit numbers. (Lessons 2.7 and 2.9)	Slate Assessment, Problem 4 Written Assessment, Problems 9 and 11–13
2h	**Developing/Secure Goal** Subtract multidigit numbers. (Lesson 2.8)	Written Assessment, Problems 10 and 14–16

Alternative Assessment

In Lesson 2.10, you will find alternative assessment options on page 150.

✦ Use +, − Fact Triangles

Use this activity from Lesson 2.1 to assess children's knowledge of addition and subtraction facts and fact families. Have children cut out Fact Triangles from *Math Masters,* pages 16 and 17. Children work in pairs. Have them sort the triangles into two piles: those facts they know and those they do not know. Consider the following questions:

• Does the child know most addition and subtraction facts?

• Which facts does the child need to practice most?

✦ Play *Name That Number* Using Multiples of 10

Use this game from Lesson 2.2 to assess children's knowledge of extended facts, as well as their skill at finding equivalent names for numbers. This game follows the rules from Lesson 1.6, except that children think of each card as a multiple of 10. For example, 5 would be 50, and 11 would be 110. You might want to have children record each number sentence on a half-sheet of paper to assess how well they are doing. Consider the following questions:

• Can the child find more than one name for a number?

• Does the child mix addition and subtraction to find names for a number?

✦ Make Up and Solve Addition and Subtraction Number Stories

Use *Math Masters,* page 21. This activity is intended to assess children's skill at writing and solving addition and subtraction number stories. Consider the following questions:

- Is the number story complete? (Is information given and a question posed?)
- Does the number story ask a question that can be answered using the information given?
- Does the number story reflect understanding of addition or subtraction?

✦ Play *Three Addends*

Use this game to assess whether children understand the concept of looking for combinations of numbers that are easy to add. *Student Reference Book,* page 234 provides the rules for this game. Consider the following questions:

- Can the child find which pair of numbers in a set of three is easiest to add?
- Does the child remember to add the third number to the sum of the pair?
- Is the child able to perform the computation mentally?

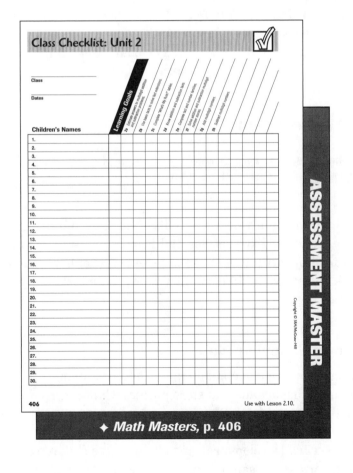

✦ *Math Masters, p. 406*

Unit 3
Assessment Overview

The focus of this unit is on linear measures and area. At this stage in their learning, children should be at a Secure level for measuring line segments to the nearest $\frac{1}{4}$ inch (see Goal 3c in the chart segment below). The chart on page 49 indicates where you can find written problems to assess children's progress toward this same goal.

Ongoing Assessment Opportunities

Ongoing assessment opportunities are opportunities to observe children during regular interactions, as they work independently and in groups. You can conduct ongoing assessment during teacher-guided instruction, Math Boxes sessions, mathematical mini-interviews, games, Mental Math and Reflexes sessions, strategy sharing, and slate work. The chart segment below suggests an ongoing assessment opportunity in Unit 3, as it relates to a specific Unit 3 learning goal.

Product Assessment Opportunities

3c **Developing/Secure Goal** Measure line segments to the nearest $\frac{1}{4}$ inch. (Lessons 3.2 and 3.3)	Lesson 3.2, p. 174

Math Journals, Math Boxes, activity sheets, masters, Math Logs, and the results of Explorations and Projects all provide product assessment opportunities. Here is an example of how you might use a rubric to assess children's ability to estimate costs and to make correct change.

Lesson 3.7, p. 201
Simulating a Shopping Trip

Children simulate a shopping trip by selecting items to buy from display ads and store posters. Children estimate the number of bills they need to give the shopkeeper and then calculate how much change they should receive. Develop a rubric to help assess children's progress, or use the sample rubric on the next page.

Periodic Assessment Opportunities

Here is a summary of the periodic assessment opportunities that are provided in Unit 3. Refer to Lesson 3.9 for details.

Oral and Slate Assessment

In Lesson 3.9, you will find oral and slate assessment problems on pages 209 and 210.

Written Assessment

In Lesson 3.9, you will find written assessment problems on page 210 (*Math Masters,* pages 374 and 375).

See the chart below to find written assessment problems that address specific learning goals.

	Goal	Written Assessment
3a	**Developing Goal** Find the perimeter of a polygon. (Lessons 3.4 and 3.5)	Written Assessment, Problems 4–6 and 9
3b	**Developing Goal** Find the area of a rectangular region divided into square units. (Lessons 3.6 and 3.7)	Written Assessment, Problems 7, 8, and 10
3c	**Developing/Secure Goal** Measure line segments to the nearest $\frac{1}{4}$ inch. (Lessons 3.2 and 3.3)	Written Assessment, Problems 1–3
3d	**Secure Goal** Measure line segments to the nearest centimeter. (Lesson 3.2)	Written Assessment, Problems 4–6

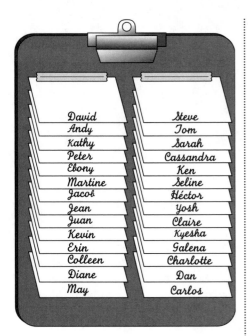

Alternative Assessment

In Lesson 3.9, you will find alternative assessment options on page 211.

✦ Find Area and Perimeter Using a Geoboard

Children use rubber bands to make various rectangles on a geoboard. Then, on a half-sheet of paper, they record the number of rows, the number of squares in each row, the area, and the perimeter. Collect the half-sheets of paper and assess how well children understand the concepts of area and perimeter. Keep such questions as the following in mind:

• Does the child find perimeter correctly?

• Does the child find area correctly?

• Is the child confusing area and perimeter?

✦ Play *Three Addends*

Circulate as children play this game. On a half-sheet of paper, have them record the order in which they added their cards. Collect the half-sheets of paper and assess children's ability to find easy combinations when adding several numbers. Keep such questions as the following in mind:

• Can the child find the pair of numbers in a set of three that is easiest to add?

• Does the child remember to add the third number to the sum of the pair?

• Is the child able to perform the computation mentally?

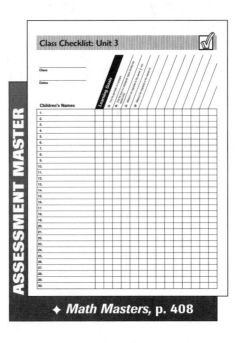

✦ *Math Masters*, p. 408

Unit 4
Assessment Overview

At this point in the *Everyday Mathematics* program, you may consider whether you are beginning to establish a balance of Ongoing, Product, and Periodic Assessment strategies. Also, think about whether your strategies include both anecdotal records based on observations of children's progress and the use of written assessments.

Ongoing Assessment Opportunities

Ongoing assessment opportunities are opportunities to observe children during regular interactions, as they work independently and in groups. You can conduct ongoing assessment during teacher-guided instruction, Math Boxes sessions, mathematical mini-interviews, games, Mental Math and Reflexes sessions, strategy sharing, and slate work. The chart below provides a summary of ongoing assessment opportunities in Unit 4, as they relate to specific Unit 4 learning goals.

4c	**Developing Goal** Know multiplication facts from the first set of Fact Triangles. (Lessons 4.5, 4.6, and 4.9)	Lesson 4.5, p. 248 Lesson 4.6, p. 257
4d	**Developing/Secure Goal** Know multiplication facts having 2, 5, or 10 as a factor. (Lessons 4.5 and 4.6)	Lesson 4.5, p. 248 Lesson 4.6, p. 257
4f	**Secure Goal** Know multiplication facts having 0 or 1 as a factor. (Lessons 4.5 and 4.6)	Lesson 4.5, p. 248 Lesson 4.6, p. 257

Product Assessment Opportunities

Math Journals, Math Boxes, activity sheets, masters, Math Logs, and the results of Explorations and Projects all provide product assessment opportunities. On the next page is an example of how you might use a rubric to assess children's ability to create and solve multiplication stories.

Lesson 4.1, p. 228
ENRICHMENT Solving Multiplication Stories

Portfolio Ideas

Circulate around the room as children work in pairs to solve multiplication number stories on journal page 83 and then make up and solve their own multiplication number stories on journal page 84. The sample rubric below can help you evaluate children's work.

Sample Rubric
Beginning (B) The child attempts to solve the multiplication number stories, but needs help filling in the multiplication/division diagram. He or she may not know how to find the necessary numbers given in the poster. In some cases, the child might fill in the numbers given on the poster but not know how to solve the problem. He or she may attempt to write the number stories, but these number stories will not be related to multiplication.
Developing (D) The child can solve most of the number-story problems on journal page 83 but has difficulty making up and solving his or her own multiplication number stories on journal page 84. The child might not be able to translate a correct number story into a diagram.
Secure (S) The child can solve the multiplication number stories on journal page 83 and successfully write and solve multiplication number stories on journal page 84. He or she may also write stories in addition to those asked for on journal page 84.

Periodic Assessment Opportunities

Here is a summary of the periodic assessment opportunities that are provided in Unit 4. Refer to Lesson 4.10 for details.

Oral and Slate Assessment

In Lesson 4.10, you will find oral and slate assessment problems on pages 277 and 278.

Written Assessment

In Lesson 4.10, you will find written assessment problems on page 277 (*Math Masters*, pages 376 and 377).

See the chart below and on the next page to find oral, slate, and written assessment problems that address specific learning goals.

4a	**Developing Goal** Solve equal grouping number stories by using multiplication. (Lessons 4.1 and 4.2)	Slate Assessment, Problem 1 Written Assessment, Problems 1 and 2
4b	**Developing Goal** Solve equal grouping and equal sharing number stories. (Lessons 4.3 and 4.4)	Slate Assessment, Problem 2 Written Assessment, Problems 3 and 4
4c	**Developing Goal** Know multiplication facts from the first set of Fact Triangles. (Lessons 4.6 and 4.9)	Slate Assessment, Problem 1 Written Assessment, Problems 1–5, 7, and 9

4d **Developing/Secure Goal** Know multiplication facts having 2, 5, or 10 as a factor. (Lessons 4.5 and 4.6)	Oral Assessment, Problems 1 and 2 Slate Assessment, Problems 1 and 3 Written Assessment, Problems 1, 5, 10, and 11	
4e **Developing/Secure Goal** Complete multiplication/division fact families. (Lessons 4.6 and 4.9)	Written Assessment, Problems 5–7	
4f **Secure Goal** Know multiplication facts having 0 or 1 as a factor. (Lesson 4.5)	Slate Assessment, Problem 1 Written Assessment, Problems 6 and 8	

Alternative Assessment

In Lesson 4.10, you will find alternative assessment options on page 278.

✦ Play *Division Arrays*

Assess children's understanding of division and remainders as they play this game. Children record each number sentence on a half-sheet of paper. If children are having difficulty, you may want them to also record the array that they made with counters. Keep the following questions in mind:

• Can the child correctly model the division situation?

• Does the child show the remainder correctly?

• Does the child write a correct number sentence for the division situation that he or she modeled?

✦ Play *Beat the Calculator*

Circulate as children play this game and have them record, on half-sheets of paper, the facts for which they did not beat the calculator. Collect the papers to assess which facts children know. Keep such questions as the following in mind as you assess children's fact power:

• Does the child know most facts?

• Which facts does the child need to practice most?

✦ Using ×, ÷ *Fact Triangles*

Circulate as children use Fact Triangles to show their knowledge of multiplication and division facts and fact families. Have children record facts that they still need to practice, and then collect their sheets. Keep such questions as the following in mind:

• Does the child know most facts?

• Which fact families are the most difficult for the child?

• Which facts does the child need to practice most?

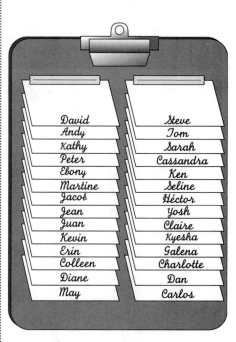

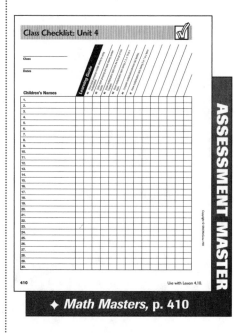

ASSESSMENT MASTER

✦ *Math Masters*, p. 410

Unit 5
Assessment Overview

A major topic of this unit is understanding and using the concept of place value in whole numbers. Children are expected to be at a Secure level for identifying place value in whole numbers up to five digits (see Goal 5h in the chart on the next page). This chart shows that ongoing assessment opportunities related to this goal can be found in Lessons 5.1 and 5.2 on pages 294 and 300 of your *Teacher's Lesson Guide*. The chart on page 56 indicates where you can find slate and written problems to help you assess children's progress toward this same goal.

Ongoing Assessment Opportunities

Ongoing assessment opportunities are opportunities to observe children during regular interactions, as they work independently and in groups. You can conduct ongoing assessment during teacher-guided instruction, Math Boxes sessions, mathematical mini-interviews, games, Mental Math and Reflexes sessions, strategy sharing, and slate work. The chart below and on the next page provides a summary of ongoing assessment opportunities in Unit 5, as they relate to specific Unit 5 learning goals.

5a **Beginning Goal** Read, write, and compare 6- and 7-digit whole numbers. (Lessons 5.3–5.5)	Lesson 5.3, p. 307 Lesson 5.5, p. 318
5b **Beginning Goal** Read and write 3-digit decimals. (Lessons 5.10 and 5.11)	Lesson 5.10, p. 348
5c **Developing Goal** Compare and order decimals. (Lessons 5.7–5.10)	Lesson 5.7, p. 329 Lesson 5.9, p. 341 Lesson 5.10, p. 348
5d **Developing Goal** Identify place value in decimals. (Lessons 5.8 and 5.9)	Lesson 5.8, p. 335 Lesson 5.9, p. 341
5e **Developing Goal** Read and write 1- and 2-digit decimals. (Lessons 5.7, 5.8, and 5.11)	Lesson 5.7, p. 327 Lesson 5.7, p. 329 Lesson 5.8, p. 335
5f **Developing/Secure Goal** Know multiplication facts from the first set of Fact Triangles. (Lessons 5.1–5.4, 5.8, and 5.12)	Lesson 5.2, p. 301 Lesson 5.3, p. 308 Lesson 5.4, p. 314 Lesson 5.8, p. 336 Lesson 5.12, p. 359

5g	**Developing/Secure Goal** Read, write, and compare whole numbers up to five digits. (Lessons 5.1–5.4 and 5.6)	Lesson 5.1, p. 293 Lesson 5.1, p. 294 Lesson 5.2, p. 300 Lesson 5.6, p. 323
5h	**Developing/Secure Goal** Identify place value in whole numbers up to five digits. (Lessons 5.1 and 5.2)	Lesson 5.1, p. 294 Lesson 5.2, p. 300

Product Assessment Opportunities

Math Journals, Math Boxes, activity sheets, masters, Math Logs, and the results of Explorations and Projects all provide product assessment opportunities. Here is an example of how you might use a rubric to assess children's understanding of tenths and hundredths.

Lesson 5.9, p 342

ENRICHMENT **Writing about Tenths and Hundredths**

Circulate and assist children as necessary as they respond to the following question: *Vanna said that 0.10 m is more than 0.2 m because 0.10 m is 10 longs but 0.2 m is 2 longs. How can you help Vanna see her mistake?* Children can respond in a Math Log (see *Math Masters* book) or on a sheet of paper. The sample rubric provided below can help you evaluate children's work.

Portfolio Ideas

Sample Rubric

Beginning (B)
The child may not understand why 0.10 m is not more than 0.2 m. With assistance, the child may be able to use base-10 blocks or a meterstick to explain why 0.2 is larger.

Developing (D)
The child can explain why 0.2 is larger than 0.1 using base-10 blocks or a meterstick. The child mentions in his or her explanation that 0.10 is equal to 1 tenth or 10 hundredths and that 0.2 is equal to 2 tenths or 20 hundredths. Some teacher assistance may be required.

Secure (S)
The child can clearly explain in writing and possibly by drawing a picture why 0.10 m is smaller than 0.2 m. The explanation might include that 0.10 m represents 1 tenth (1 long) and 0 hundredths or 10 hundredths and that 0.2 represents 2 tenths (2 longs) and 0 hundredths or 20 hundredths. The child can, therefore, conclude that 2 longs is greater than 1 long, 2 tenths is greater than 1 tenth, and 20 hundredths is greater than 10 hundredths. A picture may also be drawn to support the explanation.

Periodic Assessment Opportunities

Here is a summary of the periodic assessment opportunities that are provided in Unit 5. Refer to Lesson 5.13 for details.

Oral and Slate Assessment

In Lesson 5.13, you will find oral and slate assessment problems on pages 361 and 362.

Written Assessment

In Lesson 5.13, you will find written assessment problems on page 363 (*Math Masters*, pages 378 and 379).

See the chart below to find oral, slate, and written assessment problems that address specific learning goals.

5a **Beginning Goal** Read, write, and compare 6- and 7-digit whole numbers. (Lessons 5.3–5.5)	Oral Assessment, Problem 2 Slate Assessment, Problems 1 and 3 Written Assessment, Problem 1
5b **Beginning Goal** Read and write 3-digit decimals. (Lessons 5.10 and 5.11)	Oral Assessment, Problem 3 Slate Assessment, Problem 2
5c **Developing Goal** Compare and order decimals. (Lessons 5.7–5.9)	Written Assessment, Problems 5–7, 11, 18, and 19
5d **Developing Goal** Identify place value in decimals. (Lessons 5.8 and 5.9)	Slate Assessment, Problem 4 Written Assessment, Problems 12 and 13
5e **Developing Goal** Read and write 1- and 2-digit decimals. (Lessons 5.7, 5.8, and 5.11)	Oral Assessment, Problem 3 Slate Assessment, Problem 2 Written Assessment, Problems 2–4 and 8–10
5f **Developing/Secure Goal** Know multiplication facts from the first set of Fact Triangles. (Lessons 5.1–5.4, 5.8, and 5.12)	Written Assessment, Problems 20–37
5g **Developing/Secure Goal** Read, write, and compare whole numbers up to five digits. (Lessons 5.1–5.4 and 5.6)	Oral Assessment, Problem 2 Slate Assessment, Problem 1 Written Assessment, Problems 1, 16, and 17
5h **Developing/Secure Goal** Identify place value in whole numbers up to five digits. (Lessons 5.1 and 5.2)	Slate Assessment, Problem 3 Written Assessment, Problems 14 and 15

Alternative Assessment

In Lesson 5.13, you will find alternative assessment options on page 364.

✦ **Play** *Number Top-It*

This game is referred to in many of the lessons in Unit 5. As children play various versions of the game, use it to assess their ability to read, compare, and order 5- or 7-digit numbers and decimals to three places. Suggest that children record on a half-sheet of paper a number model (using > or <) when playing the two-players version or, if playing the more-than-two-players version, ask children to list the numbers in order from largest to smallest at the end of each round. Keep the following questions in mind:

• Does the child have an understanding of place-value concepts?

• Can the child write the numbers correctly?

• Can the child place the numbers in order from smallest to largest or largest to smallest?

✦ Play *Beat the Calculator*

As children play this game in small groups, use it to assess their fact automaticity with multiplication. As you circulate, use a Class Checklist or Flip Cards to record children's progress. You might also have children record facts on a half-sheet of paper for which they did not "beat the calculator."

✦ Use ×, ÷ Fact Triangles

As pairs of children use Fact Triangles, assess children's knowledge of multiplication and division facts and fact families. As you circulate, use a Class Checklist or Flip Cards to record children's progress. On a half-sheet of paper, you might also have children record the facts they still need to practice.

• Can the child use the fact strategies taught?

• Does the child see the relationships among fact families?

• If a child knows a multiplication fact, can he or she give the answer to a division fact within the fact family?

• Does the child have fact automaticity?

✦ *Math Masters*, p. 412

Unit 6
Assessment Overview

By the time they complete Unit 6, children should be Secure in their ability to identify and name 2- and 3-dimensional shapes. To ensure this, you might consider providing children with a variety of regular review and practice opportunities related to this skill as you move through the unit. To assess children's progress in meeting this goal (see Goal 6f in the chart below), you may wish to use the ongoing assessment suggestions on pages 409 and 438 of your *Teacher's Lesson Guide*.

Ongoing Assessment Opportunities

Ongoing assessment opportunities are opportunities to observe children during regular interactions, as they work independently and in groups. You can conduct ongoing assessment during teacher-guided instruction, Math Boxes sessions, mathematical mini-interviews, games, Mental Math and Reflexes sessions, strategy sharing, and slate work. The chart below provides a summary of ongoing assessment opportunities in Unit 6, as they relate to specific Unit 6 learning goals.

6a	**Developing Goal** Identify, draw, and name line segments, lines, and rays. (Lessons 6.1, 6.2, and 6.10)	Lesson 6.1, p. 381 Lesson 6.10, p. 432
6d	**Secure Goal** Know multiplication facts from the first set of Fact Triangles. (Lessons 6.2, 6.6–6.8, and 6.12)	Lesson 6.2, p. 387 Lesson 6.6, p. 410 Lesson 6.7, p. 416 Lesson 6.12, p. 444
6f	**Secure Goal** Identify and name 2-D and 3-D shapes. (Lessons 6.4–6.6, 6.11, and 6.12)	Lesson 6.6, p. 409 Lesson 6.11, p. 438
6g	**Secure Goal** Identify symmetric figures and draw lines of symmetry. (Lesson 6.9 and 6.11)	Lesson 6.11, p. 439

Product Assessment Opportunities

Math Journals, Math Boxes, activity sheets, masters, Math Logs, and the results of Explorations and Projects all provide product assessment opportunities. Here is an example of how you might use a rubric to assess children's ability to create an 8-point design.

Lesson 6.10, p. 431

EXPLORATION B Creating an 8-Point Design

Portfolio
Ideas

Children create an 8-point design following the directions on *Math Masters,* pages 106 and 107. Children draw several line segments from each of the points and then color the finished design. Have them do/answer the following after the design has been completed:

• Name two sets of parallel lines.

• Name at least two sets of intersecting lines.

• How many line segments are there in all?

The sample rubric below can help you evaluate children's work.

Sample Rubric
Beginning (B) The child has difficulty starting this activity independently. Most of the line segments are not straight and are often drawn to an incorrect point. Some points may be missing line segments. The child also has difficulty identifying parallel and intersecting lines and counting the number of line segments. The design is colored.
Developing (D) The child is able to complete most of the activity independently. The line segments are straight and drawn to the correct points. Most of the questions are answered, and the design is colored. The child might have difficulty answering the last question about the number of line segments. He or she may write 56, not realizing that the segments are repeats.
Secure (S) The child successfully completes the 8-point design independently. The child understands line segments and is able to generate a correct answer of 28 for the total number of line segments. The design is colored in a pattern. The child answers the questions correctly and is able to articulate his or her solution strategies.

Periodic Assessment Opportunities

Here is a summary of the periodic assessment opportunities that are provided in Unit 6. Refer to Lesson 6.13 for details.

Oral and Slate Assessment

In Lesson 6.13, you will find oral and slate assessment problems on pages 447 and 448.

Written Assessment

In Lesson 6.13, you will find written assessment problems on pages 449 (*Math Masters,* pages 380 and 381).

See the chart on the next page to find oral, slate, and written assessment problems that address specific learning goals.

6a **Developing Goal** Identify, draw, and name line segments, lines, and rays. (Lessons 6.1, 6.2, and 6.10)	Written Assessment, Problems 7–9, and 12–14
6b **Developing Goal** Draw parallel and intersecting line segments, lines, and rays. (Lesson 6.2)	Written Assessment, Problems 12–14
6c **Developing Goal** Draw angles as records of rotations. (Lesson 6.7)	Written Assessment, Problem 17
6d **Secure Goal** Know multiplication facts from the first set of Fact Triangles. (Lessons 6.2, 6.6–6.8, and 6.12)	Slate Assessment, Problem 4
6e **Developing/Secure Goal** Identify right angles. (Lessons 6.3, 6.7, and 6.8)	Slate Assessment, Problem 1 Written Assessment, Problems 11 and 15
6f **Secure Goal** Identify and name 2-D and 3-D shapes. (Lessons 6.4–6.6, 6.11, and 6.12)	Oral Assessment, Problem 1 Slate Assessment, Problems 2 and 3 Written Assessment, Problems 1–6, 9, and 10
6g **Secure Goal** Identify symmetric figures and draw lines of symmetry. (Lesson 6.9 and 6.11)	Written Assessment, Problem 16

Alternative Assessment

In Lesson 6.13, you will find alternative assessment options on page 450.

✦ Display Parallel and Intersecting Line Segments on Geoboards

Use this activity to assess children's understanding of the terms *parallel* and *intersecting*. Children use their geoboards to make a line segment and then create a line segment that intersects or is parallel to it. Have children do this activity several times, rotating between the two terms. Use your Class Checklist or Flip Cards to record children's understanding of the two terms.

✦ Create a Bulletin Board or Book of Pictures with Line Symmetry

Children in this activity create a class bulletin board or an individual book that displays pictures of objects that have line symmetry. This activity provides an opportunity for you to assess the class or individuals on their understanding of line symmetry. Children use a straightedge and marker to draw the lines of symmetry on the objects they cut out. Keep the following questions in mind as you evaluate children's work:

• Does the child's picture have line symmetry?

• Does the child correctly draw the line(s) of symmetry on the picture?

✦ Play the *Robot Game*

Use this small-group activity to assess children's understanding of rotations. Refer to the Options for Individualizing section in Lesson 6.3 for ideas. Give a group of children a set of directions to get to a destination, or invite children to write their own set of directions on a 3 × 5 inch index card. They should use turn-and-move directions. Each partner takes his or her turn as the robot and is to follow the set of directions. This is a great activity for evaluating both skill in writing directions and the ability to follow the directions.

✦ Use ×, ÷ Fact Triangles

As pairs of children use the Fact Triangles, assess children's knowledge of multiplication and division facts and fact families. As you circulate, use a Class Checklist or Flip Cards to record children's progress. You can also have children record on a half-sheet of paper the facts they still need to practice. Keep the following questions in mind:

- Can the child use the fact strategies taught?
- Does the child see the relationships among facts within the fact families?
- If a child knows a multiplication fact, can he or she give the answer to a division fact within the fact family?
- Does the child have fact automaticity?

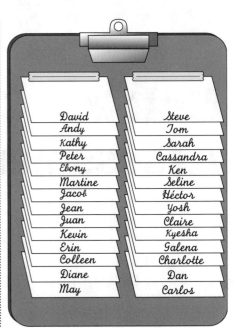

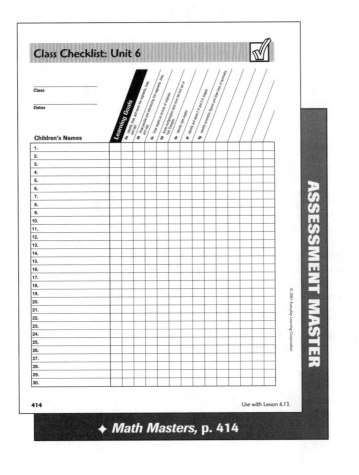

✦ *Math Masters*, p. 414

Unit 7
Assessment Overview

The focus of this unit is on multiplication and division. There are several critical abilities related to knowing and solving multiplication facts that children should be developing by this time. The goal chart below addresses these abilities (see Goals 7d and 7e) and suggests ongoing assessment opportunities that you may wish to use. Slate and written assessments for these same goals are suggested in the chart on page 64. Further, keep in mind that games are used throughout *Everyday Learning* to reinforce children's memorization of basic multiplication facts. In this unit, for example, see the references to games in the Alternative Assessment section on page 64.

Ongoing Assessment Opportunities

Ongoing assessment opportunities are opportunities to observe children during regular interactions, as they work independently and in groups. You can conduct ongoing assessment during teacher-guided instruction, Math Boxes sessions, mathematical mini-interviews, games, Mental Math and Reflexes sessions, strategy sharing, and slate work. The chart below provides a summary of ongoing assessment opportunities in Unit 7, as they relate to specific Unit 7 learning goals.

7a **Beginning/Developing Goal** Understand the function and placement of parentheses in number sentences. (Lessons 7.4 and 7.5)	Lesson 7.4, p. 551 Lesson 7.5, p. 556
7b **Beginning/Developing Goal** Make ballpark estimates for sums and products. (Lesson 7.7)	Lesson 7.7, p. 566
7d **Developing Goal** Know multiplication facts from the second set of Fact Triangles. (Lessons 7.2 and 7.3)	Lesson 7.2, p. 543
7e **Developing Goal** Solve extended multiplication facts to tens times tens. (Lessons 7.6 and 7.8)	Lesson 7.8, p. 571

Product Assessment Opportunities

Math Journals, Math Boxes, activity sheets, masters, Math Logs, and the results of Explorations and Projects all provide product assessment opportunities. Here is an example of how you might use a rubric to assess children's progress in solving ratio problems.

Lesson 7.9, p. 576

EXPLORATION B **Exploring Ratio Problems**

Children work in small groups to answer a set of questions on *Math Masters,* page 125, which explores the idea of ratio. The questions are based on the ratio of 1 cow to 7 sheep. Once finished answering the questions, group members write a report telling what they did to find the answers. Use the sample rubric below to help evaluate each group's work.

Sample Rubric

Beginning (B)
The group has difficulty starting the Seven Sheep versus One Cow problems. Teacher assistance is required. The group finds Exercises 1–3 difficult, and most of the time is spent answering these questions. Strategy sharing is not evident. Some of the answers are incorrect.

Developing (D)
The group has no difficulty starting the Seven Sheep versus One Cow problems. Children share problem solving with one another and are willing to try a variety of strategies. Group members attempt to write about their strategies but encounter some difficulty communicating their thinking. Children also include two or three of the problems that they have made up about seven sheep eating as much as one cow eats.

Secure (S)
The group can solve the Seven Sheep versus One Cow problems without teacher assistance. Children work cooperatively, using different strategies, and can articulate those strategies in the group report. Group members include three or more of the problems they have made up about seven sheep eating as much as one cow eats. The problems may also be solved.

Periodic Assessment Opportunities

Here is a summary of the periodic assessment opportunities that are provided in Unit 7. Refer to Lesson 7.10 for details.

Oral and Slate Assessment

In Lesson 7.10, you will find oral and slate assessment problems on pages 579–581.

Written Assessment

In Lesson 7.10, you will find written assessment problems on page 581 (*Math Masters,* pages 382 and 383).

See the chart below to find slate and written assessment problems that address specific learning goals.

7a	**Beginning/Developing Goal** Understand the function and placement of parentheses in number sentences. (Lessons 7.4 and 7.5)	Written Assessment, Problems 19–26
7b	**Beginning/Developing Goal** Make ballpark estimates for sums and products. (Lesson 7.7)	Written Assessment, Problems 13–18, 29, and 30
7c	**Developing Goal** Recognize and know square products. (Lessons 7.1 and 7.2)	Written Assessment, Problem 31
7d	**Developing Goal** Know multiplication facts from the second set of Fact Triangles. (Lessons 7.2 and 7.3)	Slate Assessment, Problems 1–3 Written Assessment, Problems 1–11
7e	**Developing Goal** Solve extended multiplication facts to tens × tens. (Lessons 7.6 and 7.8)	Slate Assessment, Problem 7 Written Assessment, Problems 12, 27, and 28

Alternative Assessment

In Lesson 7.10, you will find alternative assessment options on pages 581 and 582.

✦ Basketball Scores from Real Games

Children work in pairs to find possible point combinations for total scores from a real basketball game. As children solve the problems, assess their ability to insert parentheses correctly in number sentences, as well as their problem-solving skills.

• Is the partnership able to come up with several different solutions?

• Does the partnership make an organized list to keep track of the combinations?

• Does the partnership insert the parentheses in the correct places?

• Do all number sentences equal 10?

✦ Play the Extended Facts Version of *Beat the Calculator*

As children play this game in groups of three, assess how well they know fact extensions for multiplication and division. As you circulate, use a Class Checklist or Flip Cards to record children's progress.

✦ Write and Solve Problems from the Stock-Up Posters

Children write a multiplication number story using the Stock-Up Posters on pages 240 and 241 in the *Student Reference Book*. Children are asked to explain in words and with a number model how to estimate the total cost. They then calculate the actual cost using a calculator and compare their estimates to the actual total. Use this activity to assess children's ability to make reasonable estimates. Collect the stories and estimates when children have finished and keep the following questions in mind:

• Can the child write a multiplication number story that involves items from the Stock-Up Posters?

• Can the child explain how to estimate an answer to the problem, and does the number model reflect such thinking?

• Does the child make a reasonable estimate for the problem that he or she has written?

• Can the child calculate the actual cost using the calculator?

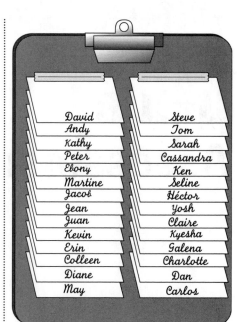

✦ Use ×, ÷ Fact Triangles

As children use the Fact Triangles in partnerships, assess their knowledge of multiplication and division facts and fact families. As you circulate, use a Class Checklist or Flip Cards to record children's progress. You can also have children record on a half-sheet of paper the facts they still need to practice. Keep the following questions in mind:

• Does the child use the fact strategies taught?

• Does the child see the relationships among the members of fact families?

• If a child knows a multiplication fact, can he or she give the answer to a division fact within the fact family?

• Does the child have fact automaticity?

✦ *Math Masters*, p. 416

Unit 8
Assessment Overview

In this unit, children further develop their ability to work with fractions. Depending on the specific skill, children's ability levels might range from Beginning to Developing. A good mix of ongoing assessment opportunities is suggested in the chart below for several learning goals that deal with fractions. Oral, written, and slate assessments for these same goals are listed in the chart on page 68.

Ongoing Assessment Opportunities

Ongoing assessment opportunities are opportunities to observe children during regular interactions, as they work independently and in groups. You can conduct ongoing assessment during teacher-guided instruction, Math Boxes sessions, mathematical mini-interviews, games, Mental Math and Reflexes sessions, strategy sharing, and slate work. The chart below provides a summary of ongoing assessment opportunities in Unit 8, as they relate to specific Unit 8 learning goals.

8a **Beginning Goal** Compare and order fractions. (Lessons 8.5 and 8.7)	Lesson 8.7, p. 632
8c **Beginning/Developing Goal** Identify fractions on a number line. (Lessons 8.3 and 8.4)	Lesson 8.3, p. 610
8d **Developing Goal** Find equivalent fractions for given fractions. (Lessons 8.1, 8.4, 8.5, and 8.6)	Lesson 8.1, p. 598 Lesson 8.4, p. 615 Lesson 8.6, p. 627
8f **Developing Goal** Identify fractional parts of a set. (Lessons 8.1, 8.3, and 8.4)	Lesson 8.3, p. 610
8g **Developing Goal** Identify fractional parts of a region. (Lessons 8.1, 8.3, and 8.5)	Lesson 8.3, p. 610

Product Assessment Opportunities

Math Journals, Math Boxes, activity sheets, masters, Math Logs, and the results of Explorations and Projects all provide product assessment opportunities. Here is an example of how you might use a rubric to assess children's ability to write and solve fraction number stories.

Lesson 8.8, p. 638

ALTERNATIVE ASSESSMENT **Write and Solve Fraction Number Stories**

Children write and solve at least two fraction number stories similar to the ones written in Lesson 8.7. They explain how they solved the fraction stories. Use this activity to assess children's understanding of fraction concepts. The sample rubric below can help you evaluate their work.

Sample Rubric

Beginning (B)
The child attempts to write a fraction story; however, he or she may connect the story to whole numbers, not to fractions. The child may write a fraction story that is difficult to solve, without that being the intention. For example, a child might write the following number story: I bought 9 apples and ate $\frac{1}{5}$ of them. How many apples did I eat? The child is unable to solve the story. He or she may try to draw a picture to illustrate the story.

Developing (D)
The child can write two fraction number stories. However, he or she may need some assistance in trying to solve a more difficult problem, such as the following: Which is more— $\frac{5}{8}$ of a candy bar or $\frac{7}{12}$ of a candy bar? The child, however, can solve easier fraction stories and explain his or her thinking.

Secure (S)
The child can write and solve at least two fraction stories independently. The fraction story may even require some higher-level thinking. For example, the fraction story may involve money, time, or measurements. The answer includes an explanation of the child's thinking. The child may also choose to illustrate the solution.

Periodic Assessment Opportunities

Here is a summary of the periodic assessment opportunities that are provided in Unit 8. Refer to Lesson 8.8 for details.

Oral and Slate Assessment

In Lesson 8.8, you will find oral and slate assessment problems on pages 635–637.

Written Assessment

In Lesson 8.8, you will find written assessment problems on pages 637 and 638 (*Math Masters,* pages 384 and 385).

See the chart on the next page to find oral, slate, and written assessment problems that address specific learning goals.

8a	**Beginning Goal** Compare and order fractions. (Lessons 8.5 and 8.7)	Oral Assessment, Problem 1 Written Assessment, Problem 8

8b	**Beginning Goal** Convert between mixed numbers and fractions. (Lesson 8.6)	Slate Assessment,
		   Problems 3 and 4
		Written Assessment,
		   Problems 9 and 10

8c	**Beginning/Developing Goal** Identify fractions on a number line. (Lessons 8.3 and 8.4)	Written Assessment, Problems 4 and 5

8d	**Developing Goal** Find equivalent fractions for given fractions. (Lessons 8.1, 8.4, 8.5, and 8.6)	Slate Assessment,
		   Problems 2 and 6
		Written Assessment,
		   Problems 6 and 7

8e	**Beginning/Developing Goal** Solve fraction number stories. (Lesson 8.7)	Slate Assessment, Problem 1 Written Assessment, Problems 11–13
8f	**Developing Goal** Identify fractional parts of a set. (Lessons 8.1 and 8.4)	Written Assessment, Problems 2 and 3
8g	**Developing Goal** Identify fractional parts of a region. (Lessons 8.1, 8.3, and 8.5)	Slate Assessment, Problem 5 Written Assessment, Problem 1

Alternative Assessment

In Lesson 8.8, you will find alternative assessment options on page 638.

✦ Play the *Equivalent Fractions Game*

As pairs of children play this game from Lesson 8.4, assess their ability to find equivalent fractions. Directions can be found in the *Student Reference Book,* page 209. As you circulate, use a Class Checklist or Flip Cards to record children's progress. You might also require that children record their pairs of equivalent fractions so that you can collect and assess the papers.

✦ Play *Fraction Top-It*

Use this game from Lesson 8.5 to assess children's understanding of comparing fractions. The directions for *Fraction Top-It* can be found on page 213 of the *Student Reference Book.* As children play the game, circulate and assess whether they understand the skills involved in comparing fractions. Keep the following questions in mind:

• Does the child select the largest fraction?

• Can the child articulate why the fraction he or she selected is larger than the other?

✦ Write and Solve Fraction Number Stories

See suggestions and the rubric given under Product Assessment Opportunities on page 67.

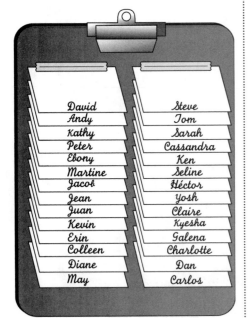

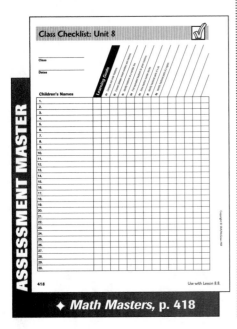

✦ *Math Masters*, p. 418

Unit 9
Assessment Overview

At this stage in *Everyday Mathematics,* children are expected to be at a Beginning/Developing level for multiplying multidigit numbers by 1- or 2-digit numbers. Because this is such a critical skill, five ongoing assessment opportunities are provided in Unit 9 (see Goal 9b in the chart below).

By this time, perhaps you have tried several different types of assessment strategies. Remember, as you use a balance of assessment approaches, the overall effectiveness of your assessment plan should improve. If there is still a major type of assessment, such as Ongoing, Product, or Periodic, that you haven't used, this unit might be a good time to try it.

Ongoing Assessment Opportunities

Ongoing assessment opportunities are opportunities to observe children during regular interactions, as they work independently and in groups. You can conduct ongoing assessment during teacher-guided instruction, Math Boxes sessions, mathematical mini-interviews, games, Mental Math and Reflexes sessions, strategy sharing, and slate work. The chart below provides a summary of ongoing assessment opportunities in Unit 9, as they relate to specific Unit 9 learning goals.

9a **Beginning Goal** Solve number stories involving positive and negative integers. (Lesson 9.13)	Lesson 9.13, p. 722
9b **Beginning/Developing Goal** Multiply multidigit numbers by 1- or 2-digit numbers. (Lessons 9.2, 9.4, 9.5, 9.9, 9.11, and 9.12)	Lesson 9.2, p. 660 Lesson 9.4, p. 672 Lesson 9.9, p. 699 Lesson 9.11, p. 710 Lesson 9.12, p. 715
9c **Beginning/Developing Goal** Find factors of a number. (Lessons 9.6 and 9.10)	Lesson 9.6, p. 681 Lesson 9.10, p. 705
9d **Beginning/Developing Goal** Interpret remainders in division problems. (Lesson 9.8)	Lesson 9.8, p. 693

Product Assessment Opportunities

Math Journals, Math Boxes, activity sheets, masters, Math Logs, and the results of Explorations and Projects all provide product assessment opportunities. Here is an example of how you might use a rubric to assess children's ability to solve equal-sharing problems.

Lesson 9.7, p. 689

EXTRA PRACTICE Sharing Money

Circulate around the room as children work in pairs to complete *Math Masters,* page 148. Children record the problem, a number model, and the answer. This activity can help you assess children's ability to solve equal-sharing problems with remainders. The sample rubric below will help you evaluate children's work.

Sample Rubric

Beginning (B)
The pair of children is able to set up the problem by rolling the die and drawing two cards. However, the number model may be written incorrectly or children may need teacher assistance. Problems b–f are difficult for partners to solve without teacher assistance. Children may get through only one of the equal-sharing problems.

Developing (D)
The pair of children sets up the problem without teacher assistance using the die and number cards. The number model is written correctly in both problems and the numbers of $10 bills and $1 bills are correct. It may be difficult for children to calculate how many cents each friend would receive if the leftover money were shared equally (Problem e). Therefore, their final answer may be incorrect.

Secure (S)
The pair of children sets up and solves the problems without teacher assistance. The number sentences are written correctly, and the numbers of $10 bills and $1 bills are correct. Children are able to calculate how the leftover money can be shared equally; thus they have a correct total for the amount that each friend would receive. Children may also be able to solve more than two problems.

Periodic Assessment Opportunities

Here is a summary of the periodic assessment opportunities that are provided in Unit 9. Refer to Lesson 9.14 for details.

Oral and Slate Assessment

In Lesson 9.14, you will find oral and slate assessment problems on pages 725–727.

Written Assessment

In Lesson 9.14, you will find written assessment problems on pages 727 and 728 (*Math Masters,* pages 386 and 387).

See the chart on the next page to find slate and written assessment problems that address specific learning goals.

9a	**Beginning Goal** Solve number stories involving positive and negative integers. (Lesson 9.13)	Written Assessment, Problem 15
9b	**Beginning/Developing Goal** Multiply multidigit numbers by 1- or 2-digit numbers. (Lessons 9.2, 9.4, 9.5, 9.9, 9.11, and 9.12)	Written Assessment, Problems 7–12
9c	**Beginning/Developing Goal** Find factors of a number. (Lessons 9.6 and 9.10)	Written Assessment, Problem 6
9d	**Beginning/Developing Goal** Interpret remainders in division problems. (Lesson 9.8)	Written Assessment, Problems 13 and 14
9e	**Developing Goal** Solve extended multiplication facts to hundreds times hundreds. (Lesson 9.1)	Slate Assessment, Problem 1 Written Assessment, Problems 1–5 and 7–10
9f	**Developing/Secure Goal** Solve equal grouping and equal sharing number stories. (Lessons 9.1, 9.5, 9.7, and 9.9)	Slate Assessment, Problem 2 Written Assessment, Problems 13 and 14

Alternative Assessment

In Lesson 9.14, you will find alternative assessment options on page 729.

✦ Play *Factor Bingo*

As children play this game from Lesson 9.6 in pairs, use it to assess their understanding of factors. As you circulate, record observations on a Class Checklist or Flip Cards to record children's progress. You may also want to invite children to write a brief summary of how they selected the numbers they chose for their Game Mat. Collect the papers when the children have finished and keep such questions as the following in mind:

• Does the child realize that certain numbers have more factors, and does he or she, therefore, continue to use them on the Game Mat?

• Does the child cover all of the numbers with the factor that is drawn from the deck?

• Does the child select numbers for the Game Mat with many factors?

• Does the child select numbers based on reasons that are not mathematical? For example, does the child select 17 because it is his or her birthday, without realizing that this number has only two factors?

✦ Share Money with Friends

See suggestions and the rubric given under Product Assessment Opportunities on page 70.

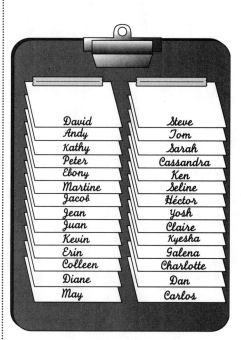

✦ *Math Masters*, p. 420

Unit 10
Assessment Overview

As you near the end of the *Third Grade Everyday Mathematics* program, reflect on your success in developing a balanced assessment plan. Think about which assessment strategies worked best. Are there strategies that you did not have time to try this year, but that you would like to try next year? To help you remember them next fall, record your thoughts on the note pages in this book.

Ongoing Assessment Opportunities

Ongoing assessment opportunities are opportunities to observe children during regular interactions, as they work independently and in groups. You can conduct ongoing assessment during teacher-guided instruction, Math Boxes sessions, mathematical mini-interviews, games, Mental Math and Reflexes sessions, strategy sharing, and slate work. The chart below provides a summary of ongoing assessment opportunities in Unit 10, as they relate to specific Unit 10 learning goals.

10a **Beginning/Developing Goal** Find the volume of rectangular prisms. (Lessons 10.2 and 10.3)	Lesson 10.2, p. 750
10b **Beginning/Developing Goal** Find the mean of a data set. (Lessons 10.7, 10.8, and 10.10)	Lesson 10.7, p. 774 Lesson 10.8, p. 779 Lesson 10.10, p. 790
10c **Developing Goal** Find the median of a data set. (Lessons 10.7 and 10.10)	Lesson 10.7, p. 775 Lesson 10.10, p. 790
10d **Developing/Secure Goal** Measure to the nearest centimeter and inch. (Lesson 10.1)	Lesson 10.1, p. 745
10e **Developing Goal** Know units of measure for length, weight, and capacity. (Lessons 10.4–10.6)	Lesson 10.4, p. 761 Lesson 10.6, p. 770
10h **Developing/Secure Goal** Make a bar graph. (Lesson 10.7)	Lesson 10.7, p. 774

Product Assessment Opportunities

Math Journals, Math Boxes, activity sheets, masters, Math Logs, and the results of Explorations and Projects all provide product assessment opportunities. Below is an example of how you might use a rubric to assess children's ability to find the volumes of cubes.

Lesson 10.2, p. 752

ENRICHMENT **Exploring the Volume of Cubes**

Children complete *Math Masters,* page 167 to find the volumes of cubes that get progressively larger. Observe to see if they can find the pattern in the sequence. Children use this pattern to find the volume of the next larger cube. The sample rubric below can help you evaluate children's progress.

Portfolio Ideas

Sample Rubric

Beginning (B)
The child may begin working on the volume activity independently and may complete Exercise 1 without teacher assistance. However, the child requires teacher guidance to complete the remainder of the page. The child has difficulty seeing the patterns that exist. Without understanding the pattern, the child also has difficulty writing an explanation for Exercise 4.

Developing (D)
The child can begin the volume activity independently. The pattern is evident to the child: The number of layers increases by 1 each time. The child may experience some difficulty writing an explanation for Exercise 4. However, he or she can make the cube.

Secure (S)
The child correctly completes the volume activity with the patterns in the sequence being quite evident. The child may also notice that the number of cubes in the layers is always a square number, such as 4, 9, 16, and 25. The child clearly articulates how he or she found the answer to Exercise 4. The child may also attempt to extend the pattern to the next several cubes.

Periodic Assessment Opportunities

Here is a summary of the periodic assessment opportunities that are provided in Unit 10. Refer to Lesson 10.12 for details.

Oral and Slate Assessment

In Lesson 10.12, you will find oral and slate assessment problems on pages 799 and 800.

Written Assessment

In Lesson 10.12, you will find written assessment problems on page 801 (*Math Masters,* pages 388 and 389).

See the chart below and on the next page to find oral, slate, and written assessment problems that address specific learning goals.

10a **Beginning/Developing Goal** Find the volume of rectangular prisms. (Lessons 10.2 and 10.3)	Written Assessment, Problem 7
10b **Beginning/Developing Goal** Find the mean of a data set. (Lessons 10.7, 10.8, and 10.10)	Written Assessment, Problem 13
10c **Developing Goal** Find the median of a data set. (Lessons 10.7 and 10.10)	Written Assessment, Problems 14 and 15

10d **Developing/Secure Goal** Measure to the nearest centimeter and inch. (Lesson 10.1)	Written Assessment, Problems 1–6
10e **Developing Goal** Know units of measure for length, weight, and capacity. (Lessons 10.4–10.6)	Written Assessment, Problems 8–11
10f **Developing/Secure Goal** Make a frequency table. (Lesson 10.10)	Written Assessment, Math Message, and Problems 13–15
10g **Developing Goal** Know multiplication facts. (Lessons 10.2, 10.5, 10.6, and 10.9)	Oral Assessment, Problem 2 Slate Assessment, Problem 2
10h **Developing/Secure Goal** Make a bar graph. (Lesson 10.7)	Written Assessment, Problem 12

Alternative Assessment

In Lesson 10.12, you will find alternative assessment options on page 802.

✦ Measure Lengths on a Treasure Hunt

As children complete *Math Masters,* page 165, assess them on their progress with respect to measuring objects to the nearest inch. Use a Class Checklist or Flip Cards to record children's progress. Keep the following questions in mind:

• Does the child use the ruler correctly? Does he or she start at 0? Does he or she use the inch side rather than the centimeter side?

• Is the child measuring each length to the nearest inch?

• Can the child find the total length of the two paths in order to determine which is shorter?

✦ Find Rectangular Prisms of a Given Volume

Use this Exploration from Lesson 10.3 to assess children's ability to find the volumes of rectangular prisms. Have children repeat the Exploration and build prisms that have a volume of 24 cubic centimeters. Children record the bases of the prisms on *Math Masters,* page 173 and create a table similar to the one on *Math Masters,* page 168, on the back. Use the following questions to help assess children's progress:

• Does the child build all of the possible prisms?

• Is the base for each prism drawn and labeled correctly?

• Is the table filled out with the correct measures?

✦ Play *Memory Addition and Subtraction*

As children play this game from Lesson 10.9, assess their understanding of how to use the memory keys on the calculator. As you circulate, use a Class Checklist or Flip Cards to record children's progress. Have children record the keystrokes they use in order to make it easier to assess how well they can use the memory keys.

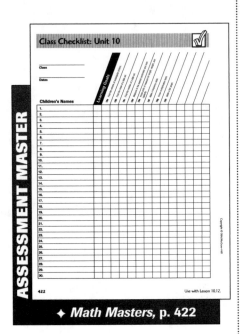

✦ *Math Masters, p. 422*

Unit 11
Assessment Overview

Looking back over the *Third Grade Everyday Mathematics* program, have you been able to establish a balance of Ongoing, Product, and Periodic Assessment strategies? Have your strategies included keeping anecdotal records based on observations of children's progress, as well as the use of written assessments? This might be a good time to evaluate your assessment strategies and think of what approaches you might consider for next year.

Ongoing Assessment Opportunities

Ongoing assessment opportunities are opportunities to observe children during regular interactions, as they work independently and in groups. You can conduct ongoing assessment during teacher-guided instruction, Math Boxes sessions, mathematical mini-interviews, games, Mental Math and Reflexes sessions, strategy sharing, and slate work. The chart below provides a summary of ongoing assessment opportunities in Unit 11, as they relate to specific Unit 11 learning goals.

11a **Developing Goal** Understand and use the language of probability. (Lessons 11.1, 11.5, and 11.7)	Lesson 11.5, p. 838 Lesson 11.7, p. 849
11c **Developing Goal** Use random draws to predict outcomes. (Lessons 11.6 and 11.7)	Lesson 11.7, p. 849
11e **Beginning/Developing Goal** Understand area model of probability and solve simple spinner problems. (Lessons 11.4, 11.5, and 11.7)	Lesson 11.5, p. 838

Product Assessment Opportunities

Math Journals, Math Boxes, activity sheets, masters, Math Logs, and the results of Explorations and Projects all provide product assessment opportunities. On the next page is an example of how you might use a rubric to assess children's understanding of probability while using spinners.

Lesson 11.5, p. 840

ENRICHMENT Designing, Describing, and Testing Spinners

Children use *Math Masters,* page 181 to make spinners of their own designs. After they design spinners, children describe how likely or unlikely it is that the spinner will land on each color. They then make 20 spins, collect the data, and write about the result. The sample rubric provided below can help you to evaluate children's progress.

Sample Rubric

Beginning (B)
The child may use only two or three colors for his or her spinner. He or she cannot describe how likely it is that the spinner will land on each color and may have difficulty recording the results of 20 spins. The child might attempt to write about the results but may have difficulty comparing his or her prediction to the actual result.

Developing (D)
The child uses six or fewer colors for his or her spinner. Next to each spinner, the child has described how likely or unlikely it is that the spinner will land on each color. The description may not be completely correct, but the child is well on his or her way to understanding the concept. The child makes 20 spins and records the outcomes. He or she answers the following question: "Did you get the results you expected?" The child may not, however, be able to explain his or her answer.

Secure (S)
The child designs the spinners using up to six colors. Next to each spinner, he or she has provided an explanation describing how likely or unlikely it is that the spinner will land on each color. The child will probably use fractions or terms like "1 out of 4" in his or her explanations. The spinners are tested with the outcomes recorded correctly. The child concludes the activity with descriptions about the expected results compared to the actual results.

Periodic Assessment Opportunities

Here is a summary of the periodic assessment opportunities that are provided for Unit 11. Refer to Lesson 11.10 for details.

Oral and Slate Assessment

In Lesson 11.10, you will find oral and slate assessment problems on pages 863–865.

Written Assessment

In Lesson 11.10, you will find written assessment problems on page 865 (*Math Masters,* pages 390 and 391).

See the chart below to find written assessment problems that address specific learning goals.

11a **Developing Goal** Understand and use the language of probability. (Lessons 11.1, 11.5, and 11.7)	Written Assessment, Problems 1 and 2
11b **Developing Goal** Use fractions to record the probabilities of events. (Lessons 11.4 and 11.5)	Written Assessment, Problem 3
11c **Developing Goal** Use random draws to predict outcomes. (Lessons 11.6 and 11.7)	Written Assessment, Problems 6 and 7

| **Developing Goal** Collect and organize data for use in predicting outcomes. (Lesson 11.7) | Written Assessment, Problems 4 and 5 |
| **Beginning/Developing Goal** Understand area model of probability and solve simple spinner problems. (Lessons 11.4, 11.5, and 11.7) | Written Assessment, Problems 2–5 |

Alternative Assessment

In Lesson 11.10, you will find alternative assessment options on page 866.

✦ **Play *Spinning to Win***

As children play this game from Lesson 11.5, assess their understanding of probability. Children determine winning strategies for the game that involves a spinner that is not divided into equal sections. Use the Class Checklist or Flip Cards to record children's thinking and strategies. You might also suggest that children write a brief summary about their winning strategies after playing several rounds. The summary should answer the question, "Which number do you think is the best pick and why?"

✦ **Play *The Block-Drawing Game***

Children play this game to explore probability. As they take turns drawing cards from the bag, they each record the information in a table. Once a child feels confident about the contents of the bag, he or she can write a prediction on his or her paper. Once all children have made their predictions, record the actual contents. Collect the papers once the game is over and keep the following questions in mind:

• Is the child's prediction reasonable?

• Does the prediction reflect the data collected in the table?

• Has the child correctly recorded the data in the table?

✦ **Calculate Travel Times**

Children use the data in the *Student Reference Book,* page 267 to generate two number stories involving elapsed time. In Lesson 11.8, children solved similar number stories. Collect the stories when children have finished to assess their progress on understanding the concept of elapsed time. Keep the following questions in mind:

• Does the child write number stories that require finding elapsed time?

• Does each number story end with a question?

• Does the child solve the number stories by calculating the elapsed time?

• When calculating the elapsed time, does the child still require the use of a clock, or does the child use other strategies?

✦ *Math Masters*, p. 424

ASSESSMENT MASTER

Assessment Masters

How to Use the Masters

The *Assessment Handbook* contains reduced versions of all of the Assessment Masters found in your *Math Masters* book. You can use these reduced pages to assist you in developing your assessment plan. The following general masters may be adapted in any way to suit your needs; however, the suggestions below may be helpful.

Use the **List of Assessment Sources** to keep track of the sources that you are currently using. As you plan your assessment, aim for the balance of techniques that will meet your children's needs.

On the **Individual Profile of Progress**

• Copy the Learning Goals from the Review and Assessment Lesson at the end of each unit. (See the *Teacher's Lesson Guide.*)

• Make as many copies of the form as you need for each child in your class.

• Keep track of each child's progress on each unit's skills and concepts using this form.

• Check whether each child is Beginning, Developing, or Secure in each of the content areas.

• You may alternatively wish to use the **Class Checklist.**

Make several copies of the **Class Progress Indicator.** Use one page for each mathematical topic being assessed. Fill in the topic you wish to assess under the chart heading and then write each child's name in the appropriate box, indicating whether he or she is Beginning, Developing, or Secure.

The **Parent Reflections** master can be sent to parents prior to parent conferences, so that parents can identify their concerns prior to the meeting.

You can use the **Rubric** master to create your own rubric for a given task, especially for products that will be included in portfolios. Use Beginning, Developing, Secure or your own rubric scheme.

All of the other forms are to be passed out to children. Use the interest inventories to find out how children feel about mathematics. Self-assessment forms should be used as attachments to portfolio items. The remaining forms can provide insight into how comfortable children feel with the math content.

NOTE: This page provides a brief summary of how the general Assessment Masters may be used. The uses of these masters are described in more detail near the front of this book on pages 5–34.

Name **Date** **Time**

Unit 1 Checking Progress

Fill in the missing numbers.

1.

35	36
45	
55	

2.

	85	
94	95	96
		105

3.

193		195
	204	
213		215

4. Draw coins to show 58¢ two ways. Use ⓟ, ⓝ, ⓓ, and ⓠ.

Sample answers: ⓠ ⓠ ⓝ ⓟ ⓟ ⓟ | ⓠ ⓓ ⓓ ⓟ ⓟ ⓟ

5. Tim bought a 55¢ bag of chips. He put 3 quarters in the vending machine.

a. How much money did he get back? __20¢__

b. Draw the coins he might get back. Use ⓝ, ⓓ, and ⓠ.

Possible answers:
ⓝ ⓝ ⓝ ⓝ or ⓓ ⓓ or ⓓ ⓝ ⓝ

c. What is the smallest number of coins he could get back? __2 coins__

6. Cross out three names that do not belong. Write the name on the tag. Add one more correct name to the box.

20	
10 twos	10 + 10
half of 40	~~25 − 20~~
~~1 dozen + 6~~	~~10 + 10 + 10~~
ten less than 30	3 + 3 + 3 + 10 + 1

Use with Lesson 1.13.

369

Name **Date** **Time**

Unit 1 Checking Progress (cont.)

7. Write the number that is 10 more than 195. __205__

8. Write the number that is 100 less than 3,802. __3,702__

9. Write the number that is 1,000 more than 482. __1,482__

Draw the minute hand and hour hand to show the times.

10.

3:15

11.

7:55

12.

10:32

13. Fill in the missing numbers.

Rule
+10

24 → 34 → 44 → 54 → 64 → 74

14. Fill in the missing rule and the missing numbers.

Rule
+3

21 → 24 → 27 → 30 → 33 → 36

15. Use some or all the cards below to write as many different names as you can for the target number.

3	7
4	2
	5

9
target number

Sample answers: 7 + 2, 3 + 4 + 2,
7 + 4 − 2, 5 + 4, 3 + 4 + 7 − 5

Use with Lesson 1.13.

370

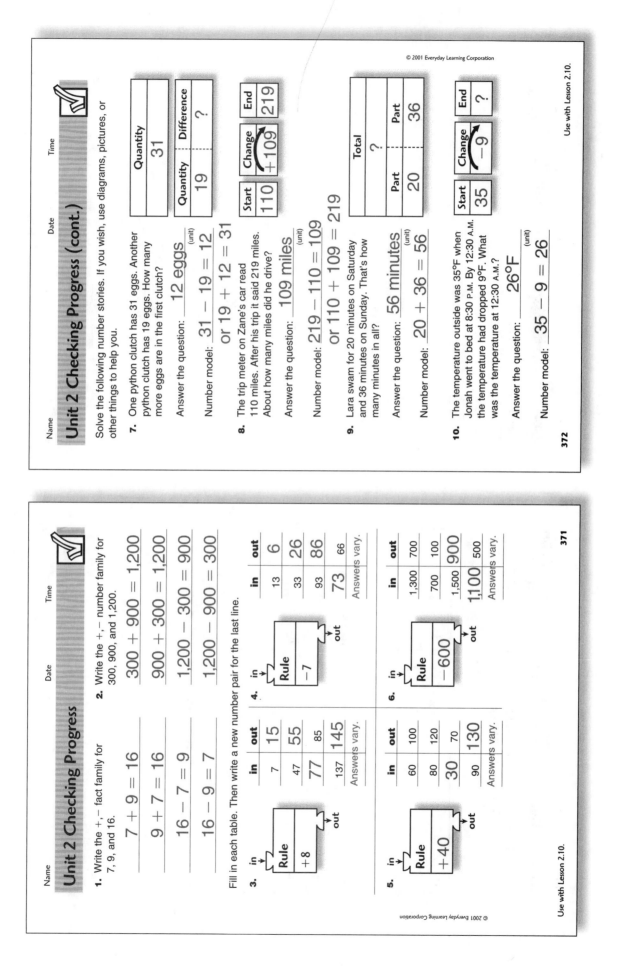

Name _____ Date _____ Time _____

Unit 2 Checking Progress

1. Write the +, − fact family for 7, 9, and 16.

7 + 9 = 16
9 + 7 = 16
16 − 7 = 9
16 − 9 = 7

2. Write the +, − number family for 300, 900, and 1,200.

300 + 900 = 1,200
900 + 300 = 1,200
1,200 − 300 = 900
1,200 − 900 = 300

Fill in each table. Then write a new number pair for the last line.

3. Rule +8

in	out
7	15
47	55
77	85
137	145

Answers vary.

4. Rule −7

in	out
13	6
33	26
93	86
73	66

Answers vary.

5. Rule +40

in	out
60	100
80	120
30	70
90	130

Answers vary.

6. Rule −600

in	out
1,300	700
700	100
1,500	900
1,100	500

Answers vary.

Use with Lesson 2.10.

371

Name _____ Date _____ Time _____

Unit 2 Checking Progress (cont.)

Solve the following number stories. If you wish, use diagrams, pictures, or other things to help you.

7. One python clutch has 31 eggs. Another python clutch has 19 eggs. How many more eggs are in the first clutch?

Quantity
31

Quantity	Difference
19	?

Answer the question: __12 eggs__ (unit)

Number model: 31 − 19 = 12
or 19 + 12 = 31

8. The trip meter on Zane's car read 110 miles. After his trip it said 219 miles. About how many miles did he drive?

Start	Change	End
110	+109	219

Answer the question: __109 miles__ (unit)

Number model: 219 − 110 = 109
or 110 + 109 = 219

9. Lara swam for 20 minutes on Saturday and 36 minutes on Sunday. That's how many minutes in all?

Total
?

Part	Part
20	36

Answer the question: __56 minutes__ (unit)

Number model: 20 + 36 = 56

10. The temperature outside was 35°F when Jonah went to bed at 8:30 P.M. By 12:30 A.M. the temperature had dropped 9°F. What was the temperature at 12:30 A.M.?

Start	Change	End
35	−9	?

Answer the question: __26°F__ (unit)

Number model: 35 − 9 = 26

Use with Lesson 2.10.

372

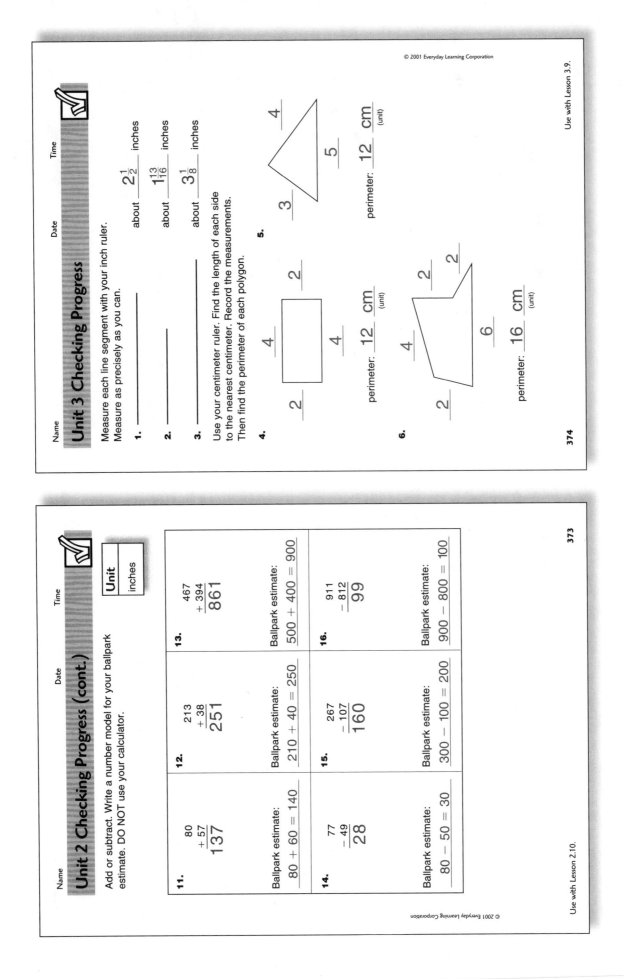

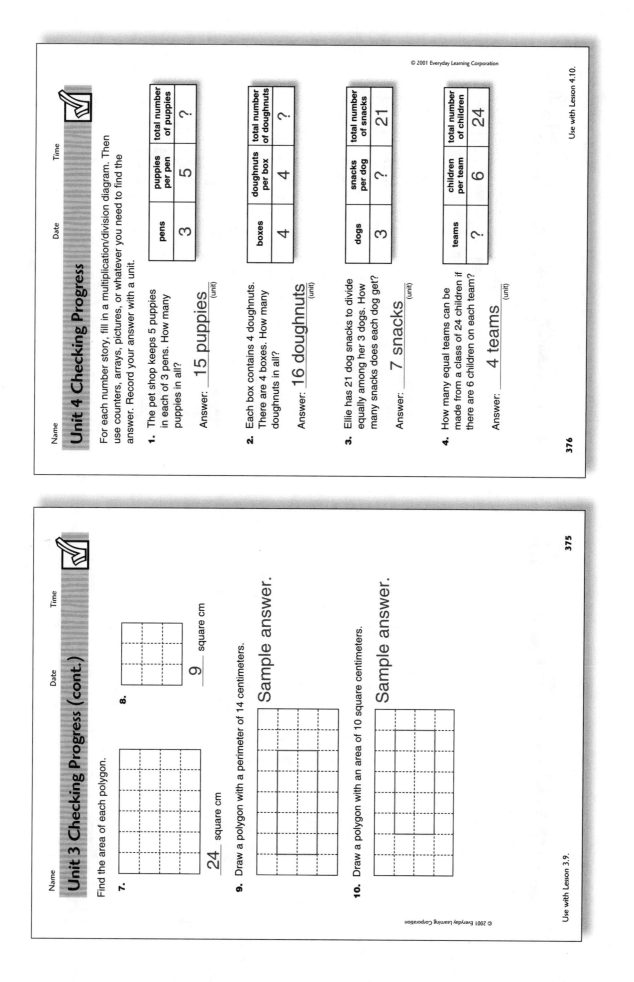

Unit 4 Checking Progress

For each number story, fill in a multiplication/division diagram. Then use counters, arrays, pictures, or whatever you need to find the answer. Record your answer with a unit.

1. The pet shop keeps 5 puppies in each of 3 pens. How many puppies in all?

pens	puppies per pen	total number of puppies
3	5	?

Answer: __15 puppies__ (unit)

2. Each box contains 4 doughnuts. There are 4 boxes. How many doughnuts in all?

boxes	doughnuts per box	total number of doughnuts
4	4	?

Answer: __16 doughnuts__ (unit)

3. Ellie has 21 dog snacks to divide equally among her 3 dogs. How many snacks does each dog get?

dogs	snacks per dog	total number of snacks
3	?	21

Answer: __7 snacks__ (unit)

4. How many equal teams can be made from a class of 24 children if there are 6 children on each team?

teams	children per team	total number of children
?	6	24

Answer: __4 teams__ (unit)

Use with Lesson 4.10.

376

Unit 3 Checking Progress (cont.)

Find the area of each polygon.

7.

__24__ square cm

8.

__9__ square cm

9. Draw a polygon with a perimeter of 14 centimeters.

Sample answer.

10. Draw a polygon with an area of 10 square centimeters.

Sample answer.

Use with Lesson 3.9.

375

Unit 5 Checking Progress

Name _____ Date _____ Time _____

Circle the largest number. Underline the smallest number.

1.
| 347,268 | 35,926 | 78,613 | 309,827 | 106,208 |
| 298,472 | 39,562 | 16,209 | 160,028 | (350,142) |

If each grid is ONE, then what part of each grid is shaded? Write a decimal below each grid.

2. 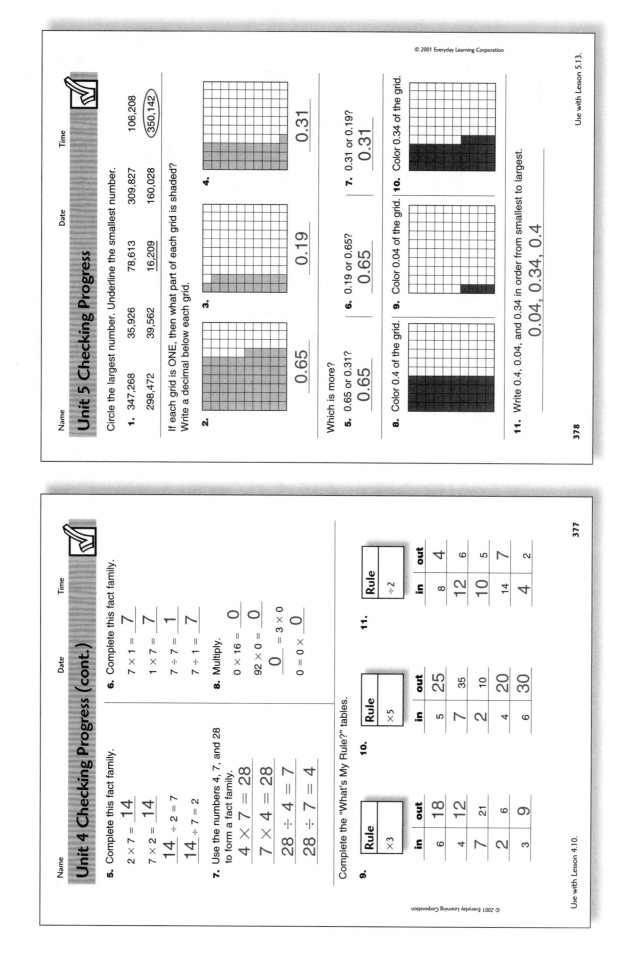 0.65

3. 0.19

4. 0.31

Which is more?

5. 0.65 or 0.31?   0.65

6. 0.19 or 0.65?   0.65

7. 0.31 or 0.19?   0.31

8. Color 0.4 of the grid.

9. Color 0.04 of the grid.

10. Color 0.34 of the grid.

11. Write 0.4, 0.04, and 0.34 in order from smallest to largest.
0.04, 0.34, 0.4

Use with Lesson 5.13.

Unit 4 Checking Progress (cont.)

Name _____ Date _____ Time _____

5. Complete this fact family.
2 × 7 = 14
7 × 2 = 14
14 ÷ 2 = 7
14 ÷ 7 = 2

6. Complete this fact family.
7 × 1 = 7
1 × 7 = 7
7 ÷ 7 = 1
7 ÷ 1 = 7

7. Use the numbers 4, 7, and 28 to form a fact family.
4 × 7 = 28
7 × 4 = 28
28 ÷ 4 = 7
28 ÷ 7 = 4

8. Multiply.
0 × 16 = 0
92 × 0 = 0
0 = 3 × 0
0 = 0 × 0

Complete the "What's My Rule?" tables.

9.
Rule ×3	
in	out
6	18
4	12
7	21
2	6
3	9

10.
Rule ×5	
in	out
5	25
7	35
2	10
4	20
6	30

11.
Rule ÷2	
in	out
8	4
12	6
10	5
14	7
4	2

Use with Lesson 4.10.

Name

Date

Time

Unit 6 Checking Progress

Fill in the ovals to show your answers. There is more than one correct answer for some items, so you may need to fill in more than one oval.

1.

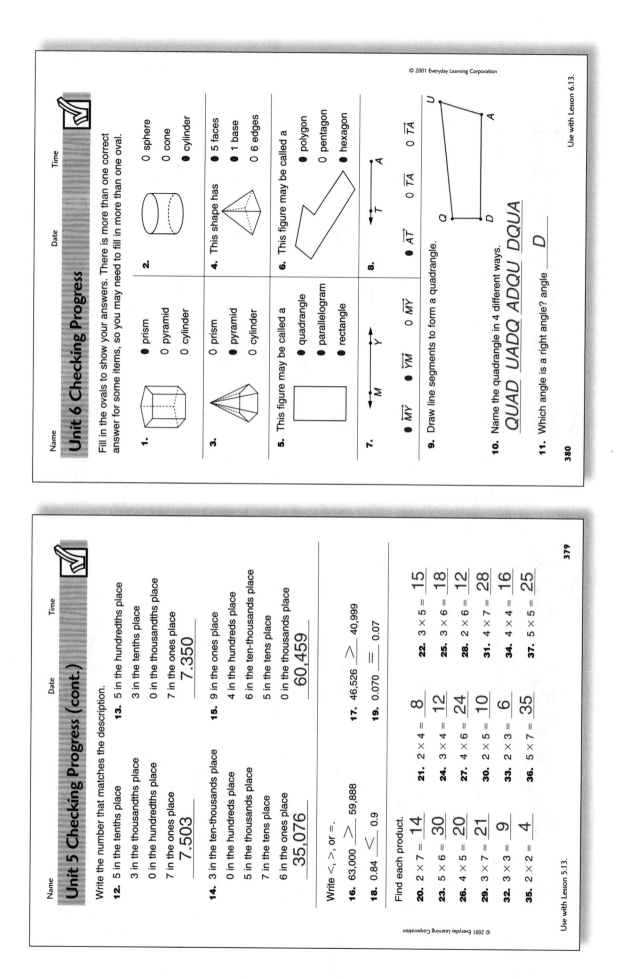

● prism
○ pyramid
○ cylinder

2.

○ sphere
○ cone
● cylinder

3.

○ prism
● pyramid
○ cylinder

4. This shape has

● 5 faces
● 1 base
● 6 edges

5. This figure may be called a

● quadrangle
● parallelogram
● rectangle

6. This figure may be called a

● polygon
○ pentagon
● hexagon

7.

● $\overrightarrow{MY}$ ● $\overrightarrow{YM}$ ○ $\overrightarrow{MY}$

8.

● $\overrightarrow{AT}$ ○ $\overline{TA}$ ○ $\overrightarrow{TA}$

9. Draw line segments to form a quadrangle.

10. Name the quadrangle in 4 different ways.

QUAD   UADQ   ADQU   DQUA

11. Which angle is a right angle? angle ___D___

380

Use with Lesson 6.13.

Name

Date

Time

Unit 5 Checking Progress (cont.)

Write the number that matches the description.

12. 5 in the tenths place
3 in the thousandths place
0 in the hundredths place
7 in the ones place

___7.503___

13. 5 in the hundredths place
3 in the tenths place
0 in the thousandths place
7 in the ones place

___7.350___

14. 3 in the ten-thousands place
0 in the hundreds place
5 in the thousands place
7 in the tens place
6 in the ones place

___35,076___

15. 9 in the ones place
4 in the hundreds place
6 in the ten-thousands place
5 in the tens place
0 in the thousands place

___60,459___

Write <, >, or =.

16. 63,000 $>$ 59,888

17. 46,526 $>$ 40,999

18. 0.84 $<$ 0.9

19. 0.070 $=$ 0.07

Find each product.

20. $2 \times 7 =$ __14__

21. $2 \times 4 =$ __8__

22. $3 \times 5 =$ __15__

23. $5 \times 6 =$ __30__

24. $3 \times 4 =$ __12__

25. $3 \times 6 =$ __18__

26. $4 \times 5 =$ __20__

27. $4 \times 6 =$ __24__

28. $2 \times 6 =$ __12__

29. $3 \times 7 =$ __21__

30. $2 \times 5 =$ __10__

31. $4 \times 7 =$ __28__

32. $3 \times 3 =$ __9__

33. $2 \times 3 =$ __6__

34. $4 \times 4 =$ __16__

35. $2 \times 2 =$ __4__

36. $5 \times 7 =$ __35__

37. $5 \times 5 =$ __25__

379

Use with Lesson 5.13.

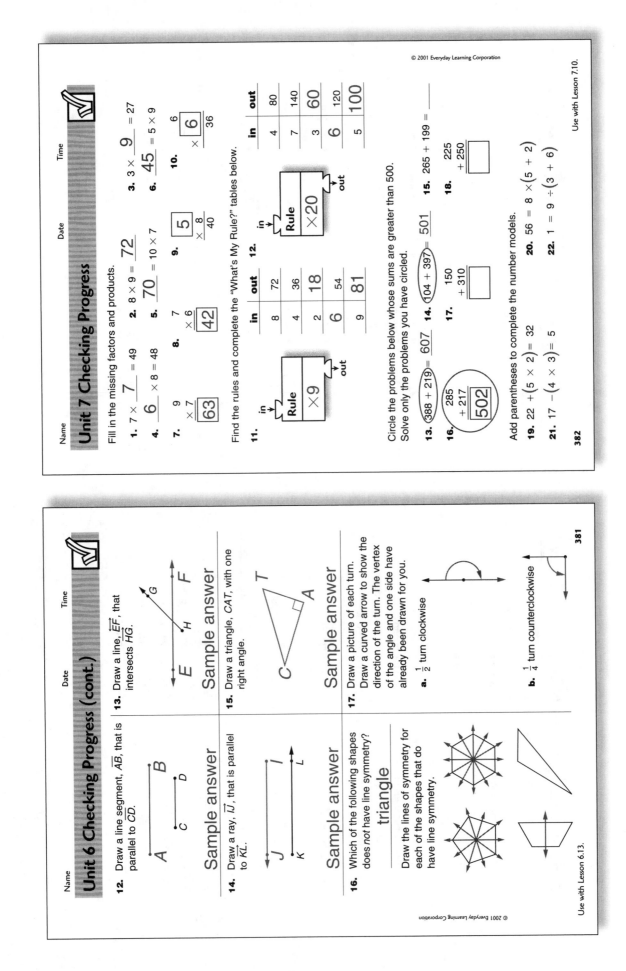

Unit 6 Checking Progress (cont.)

Name Date Time

12. Draw a line segment, $\overline{AB}$, that is parallel to $\overline{CD}$.

A ——— B
C — D

Sample answer

13. Draw a line, $\overleftrightarrow{EF}$, that intersects $\overrightarrow{HG}$.

E — F
H G

Sample answer

14. Draw a ray, $\overrightarrow{IJ}$, that is parallel to $\overrightarrow{KL}$.

I — J
K — L

Sample answer

15. Draw a triangle, *CAT*, with one right angle.

C A T

Sample answer

16. Which of the following shapes does *not* have line symmetry?

triangle

Draw the lines of symmetry for each of the shapes that do have line symmetry.

17. Draw a picture of each turn. Draw a curved arrow to show the direction of the turn. The vertex of the angle and one side have already been drawn for you.

a. $\frac{1}{2}$ turn clockwise

b. $\frac{1}{4}$ turn counterclockwise

Use with Lesson 6.13.

© 2001 Everyday Learning Corporation

381

Unit 7 Checking Progress

Name Date Time

Fill in the missing factors and products.

1. $7 \times 7 = 49$
2. $8 \times 9 = 72$
3. $3 \times 9 = 27$
4. $6 \times 8 = 48$
5. $70 = 10 \times 7$
6. $45 = 5 \times 9$

7. $\begin{array}{r} 9 \\ \times 7 \\ \hline 63 \end{array}$
8. $\begin{array}{r} 7 \\ \times 6 \\ \hline 42 \end{array}$
9. $\begin{array}{r} 5 \\ \times 8 \\ \hline 40 \end{array}$
10. $\begin{array}{r} 6 \\ \times 6 \\ \hline 36 \end{array}$

Find the rules and complete the "What's My Rule?" tables below.

11. Rule ×9

in	out
8	72
4	36
2	18
6	54
9	81

12. Rule ×20

in	out
4	80
7	140
3	60
6	120
5	100

Circle the problems below whose sums are greater than 500. Solve only the problems you have circled.

13. (388 + 219) = 607
14. (104 + 397) = 501
15. 265 + 199 =

16. $\begin{array}{r} 285 \\ + 217 \\ \hline 502 \end{array}$
17. $\begin{array}{r} 150 \\ + 310 \\ \hline \end{array}$
18. $\begin{array}{r} 225 \\ + 250 \\ \hline \end{array}$

Add parentheses to complete the number models.

19. $22 + (5 \times 2) = 32$
20. $56 = 8 \times (5 + 2)$
21. $17 - (4 \times 3) = 5$
22. $1 = 9 \div (3 + 6)$

Use with Lesson 7.10.

382

© 2001 Everyday Learning Corporation

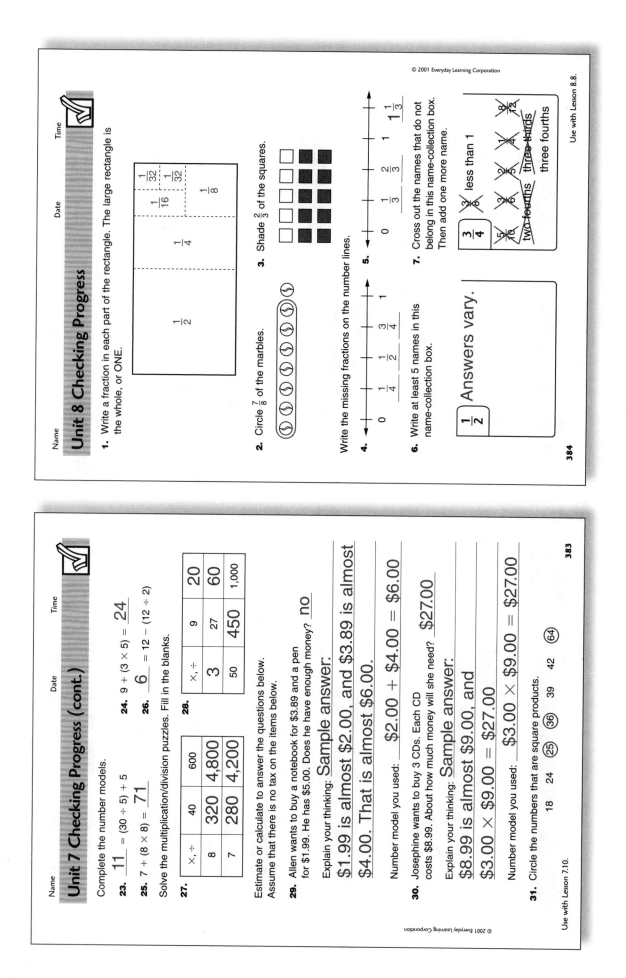

Unit 8 Checking Progress

© 2001 Everyday Learning Corporation

1. Write a fraction in each part of the rectangle. The large rectangle is the whole, or ONE.

$\frac{1}{2}$	$\frac{1}{4}$ $\frac{1}{16}$ $\frac{1}{32}$
	$\frac{1}{8}$ $\frac{1}{32}$

2. Circle $\frac{7}{8}$ of the marbles.

3. Shade $\frac{2}{3}$ of the squares.

Write the missing fractions on the number lines.

4. $0 \quad \frac{1}{4} \quad \frac{1}{2} \quad \frac{3}{4} \quad 1$

5. $0 \quad \frac{1}{3} \quad \frac{2}{3} \quad 1 \quad 1\frac{1}{3}$

6. Write at least 5 names in this name-collection box.

$\frac{1}{2}$
Answers vary.

7. Cross out the names that do not belong in this name-collection box. Then add one more name.

$\frac{3}{4}$
$\frac{3}{8}$ $\frac{3}{4}$ less than 1
$\frac{5}{16}$ $\frac{2}{6}$ $\frac{6}{8}$ $\frac{8}{12}$
two-fourths three-thirds
three fourths

384 Use with Lesson 8.8.

Unit 7 Checking Progress (cont.)

Complete the number models.

23. $\underline{11} = (30 \div 5) + 5$

24. $9 + (3 \times 5) = \underline{24}$

25. $7 + (8 \times 8) = \underline{71}$

26. $\underline{6} = 12 - (12 \div 2)$

Solve the multiplication/division puzzles. Fill in the blanks.

27.

×, ÷	40	600
8	320	4,800
7	280	4,200

28.

×, ÷	9	20
3	27	60
50	450	1,000

Estimate or calculate to answer the questions below. Assume that there is no tax on the items below.

29. Allen wants to buy a notebook for $3.89 and a pen for $1.99. He has $5.00. Does he have enough money? __no__

Explain your thinking: Sample answer: $1.99 is almost $2.00, and $3.89 is almost $4.00. That is almost $6.00.

Number model you used: __$2.00 + $4.00 = $6.00.__

30. Josephine wants to buy 3 CDs. Each CD costs $8.99. About how much money will she need? __$27.00__

Explain your thinking: Sample answer: $8.99 is almost $9.00, and $3.00 × $9.00 = $27.00

Number model you used: __$3.00 × $9.00 = $27.00__

31. Circle the numbers that are square products.

18 24 ⑤ ㊱ 39 42 ㊸

Use with Lesson 7.10. 383

Unit 8 Checking Progress (cont.)

Name _____ Date _____ Time _____

8. Circle all of the fractions below that are greater than $\frac{3}{4}$.

$\frac{2}{3}$ $\frac{1}{4}$ $\left(\frac{4}{5}\right)$ $\frac{2}{9}$ $\frac{4}{10}$ $\frac{7}{12}$ $\left(\frac{7}{8}\right)$ $\left(\frac{5}{4}\right)$

Shade the circles to match the mixed number or fraction.

9. $\frac{9}{5}$ Write another name for $\frac{9}{5}$. $1\frac{4}{5}$

10. $2\frac{3}{4}$ Write another name for $2\frac{3}{4}$. $\frac{11}{4}$

11. Jolene had 8 pieces of candy. She divided the candy equally among herself and 3 friends. How many pieces of candy did each person get? ___2___ pieces

What fraction of the candy did Jolene get? $\frac{1}{4}$

12. Lora's mom gave her $\frac{3}{4}$ of a dollar to buy a drink.
Joe's mom gave him $\frac{4}{5}$ of a dollar to buy a drink.
Who got more money? ___Joe___

Explain how you got your answer. Sample answer: $\frac{3}{4}$ of a dollar is 75¢; $\frac{4}{5}$ of a dollar is 80¢. 80¢ is more than 75¢.

13. Mark saved his allowance for 3 weeks. He spent $\frac{2}{3}$ of his money on a movie. The movie cost $6. How much money did he have left? $ ___3___

Use with Lesson 8.8.

© 2001 Everyday Learning Corporation

385

Unit 9 Checking Progress

Name _____ Date _____ Time _____

© 2001 Everyday Learning Corporation

Multiply.

1. a. $20 \times 30 =$ ___600___
   b. $20 \times 300 =$ ___6,000___

2. a. $40\ [50s] =$ ___2,000___
   b. $40\ [500s] =$ ___20,000___

3. How many 6s are there in 240? ___40___

4. How many 60s are there in 2,400? ___40___

5. How much do four 180-pound pumas weigh? ___720___ pounds

Explain how you got your answer.
Sample answer: $4 \times 180 =$
$4\ [100] + 4\ [80] = 400 + 320 = 720$

6. This is part of a *Factor Bingo* game mat. Put an X on the square you could cover if you turned over a 4.

15	21	30
~~32~~	50	27
43	82	70

Multiply. Fill in the missing numbers. Use the partial-products algorithm.

7.
```
    3 8
  × 5 0
  1 5 0 0
+   4 0 0
  1 9 0 0
```

8.
```
    2 7
  × 4 6
    8 0 0
    2 8 0
    1 2 0
  +   4 2
  1 2 4 2
```

9.
```
    9 3 6
  ×     4
  3 6 0 0
    1 2 0
      2 4
+  3 7 4 4
```

10.
```
    6 8
  × 3 5
  1 8 0 0
    2 4 0
    3 0 0
  +   4 0
  2 3 8 0
```

Use with Lesson 9.14.

386

Unit 9 Checking Progress (cont.)

Name _____ Date _____ Time _____

Multiply. Use the lattice method.

11. $42 \times 17 =$ ___714___

12. $306 \times 30 =$ ___9,180___

13. Marge is buying hamburger buns for Family Math Night. She needs 150 buns. They come in packages of 8. How many packages should she buy? ___19___ packages

Explain how you got your answer: __Sample answer: $8 \times 20 = 160$,__
__so 20 packages is too many. 19 packages $= 160 - 8 = 152$__
__buns. This is 2 extra.__

14. $84 is shared equally by 5 friends.

a. How many $10 bills does each friend get? ___1___ $10 bill(s)

b. How many $1 bills does each friend get? ___6___ $1 bill(s)

c. How many $1 bills are left over? ___4___ $1 bill(s)

d. If the leftover money is shared equally, how many cents does each friend get? ___$0.80___

e. Each friend gets a total of ___$16.80___

f. Number model: __$84 \div 5 = $16.80__

15. In the morning, it was −3°F. By noon, it had warmed up to 14°F. How much warmer was it at noon than in the morning? ___17___ °

Explain how you worked: __Sample answer: From 3° below 0 to 0__
__is 3 steps; from 0 to 14 is 14 steps. So, $3 + 14 = 17$.__

Use with Lesson 9.14.

387

Unit 10 Checking Progress

Name _____ Date _____ Time _____

1. Make a dot at $2\frac{1}{2}$ inches. Label it with the letter A.

2. Make a dot at $4\frac{1}{4}$ inches. Label it with the letter B.

3. Make a dot at $5\frac{3}{8}$ inches. Label it with the letter C.

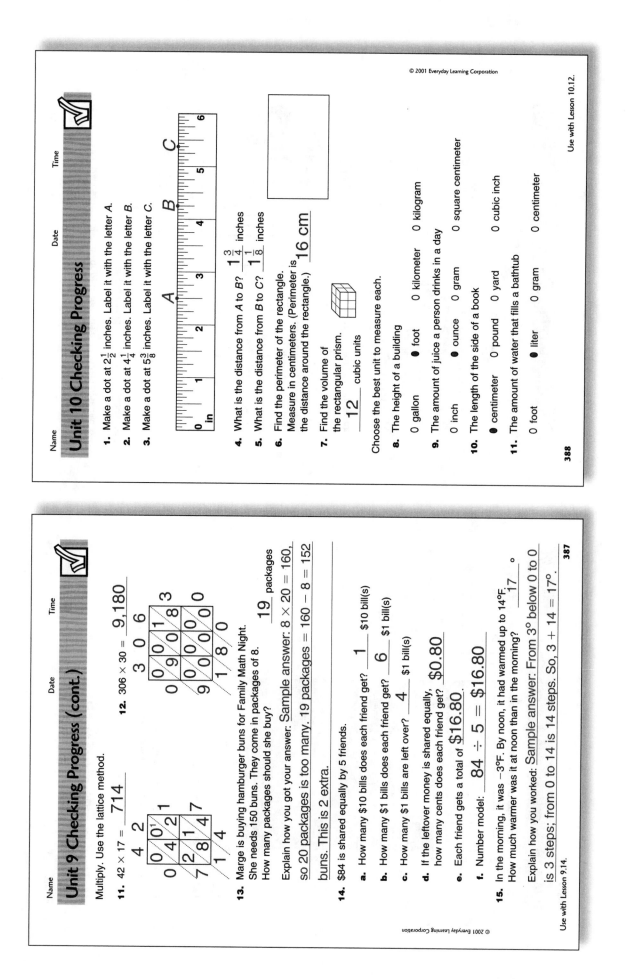

4. What is the distance from A to B? $1\frac{3}{4}$ inches

5. What is the distance from B to C? $1\frac{1}{8}$ inches

6. Find the perimeter of the rectangle. Measure in centimeters. (Perimeter is the distance around the rectangle.) ___16 cm___

7. Find the volume of the rectangular prism. ___12___ cubic units

Choose the best unit to measure each.

8. The height of a building
○ gallon ● foot ○ kilometer ○ kilogram

9. The amount of juice a person drinks in a day
○ inch ● ounce ○ gram ○ square centimeter

10. The length of the side of a book
● centimeter ○ pound ○ yard ○ cubic inch

11. The amount of water that fills a bathtub
○ foot ● liter ○ gram ○ centimeter

Use with Lesson 10.12.

388

Name _____ Date _____ Time _____

Unit 11 Checking Progress

1. Write the letter of the best description for each event.

   C A coin will land heads-up.

   d A house on your street will catch on fire today.

   e A cow will fly.

   a It will rain at least once this year.

   b A person will be warm if he or she wears a winter coat.

   a. Sure

   b. Likely

   c. 50/50

   d. Unlikely

   e. Impossible

2. Shade the oval next to each statement that is true for the spinner below.

   O You are half as likely to get white as black.

   O You are 2 times as likely to get dots as white.

   ● You are likely to get stripes or black a little more than $\frac{1}{2}$ of the time.

   ● You will get dots about $\frac{1}{4}$ of the time.

   O You have about the same chance of getting stripes or black.

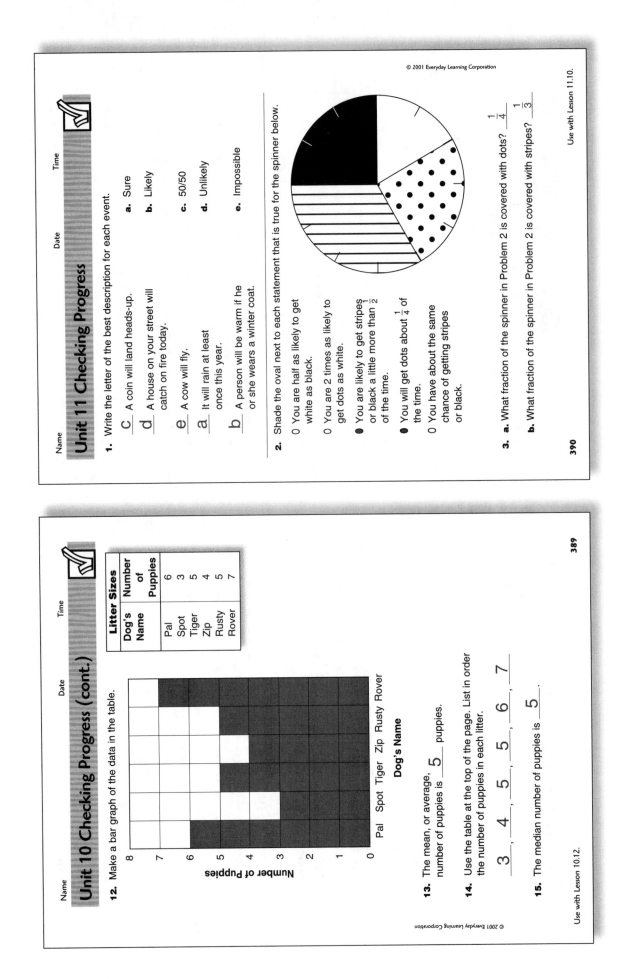

3. a. What fraction of the spinner in Problem 2 is covered with dots? $\frac{1}{4}$

   b. What fraction of the spinner in Problem 2 is covered with stripes? $\frac{1}{3}$

Use with Lesson 11.10.

390

Name _____ Date _____ Time _____

Unit 10 Checking Progress (cont.)

Litter Sizes

Dog's Name	Number of Puppies
Pal	6
Spot	3
Tiger	5
Zip	4
Rusty	5
Rover	7

12. Make a bar graph of the data in the table.

Number of Puppies (0–8)

Dog's Name: Pal Spot Tiger Zip Rusty Rover

13. The mean, or average, number of puppies is 5 puppies.

14. Use the table at the top of the page. List in order the number of puppies in each litter.

    3 , 4 , 5 , 5 , 6 , 7

15. The median number of puppies is 5 .

Use with Lesson 10.12.

389

Name _____ Date _____ Time _____

Midyear Assessment

Complete each count.

1. 25, 50, _75_ , _100_ , 125 , _150_

2. 100, _200_ , 300, 400, _500_ , _600_

3. 1,470, _1,570_ , 1,670 , _1,770_ , 1,870 , _1,970_

4. Use the number 34,892.

Which digit is in the tens place? _9_

Which digit is in the hundreds place? _8_

Which digit is in the ten-thousands place? _3_

What is the smallest 5-digit number you
can make with the digits 3, 4, 8, 9, and 2? _23,489_

5.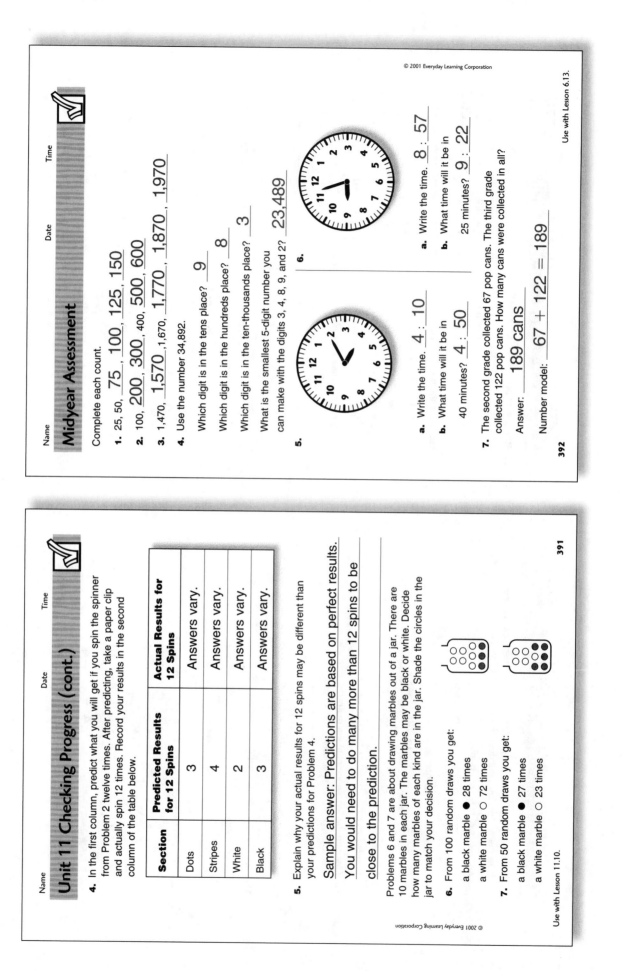

a. Write the time. _4_ : _10_

b. What time will it be in
40 minutes? _4_ : _50_

6.

a. Write the time. _8_ : _57_

b. What time will it be in
25 minutes? _9_ : _22_

7. The second grade collected 67 pop cans. The third grade
collected 122 pop cans. How many cans were collected in all?

Answer: _189 cans_

Number model: _67 + 122 = 189_

Use with Lesson 6.13.

Name _____ Date _____ Time _____

Unit 11 Checking Progress (cont.)

4. In the first column, predict what you will get if you spin the spinner
from Problem 2 twelve times. After predicting, take a paper clip
and actually spin 12 times. Record your results in the second
column of the table below.

Section	Predicted Results for 12 Spins	Actual Results for 12 Spins
Dots	3	Answers vary.
Stripes	4	Answers vary.
White	2	Answers vary.
Black	3	Answers vary.

5. Explain why your actual results for 12 spins may be different than
your predictions for Problem 4.

Sample answer: Predictions are based on perfect results.

You would need to do many more than 12 spins to be

close to the prediction.

Problems 6 and 7 are about drawing marbles out of a jar. There are
10 marbles in each jar. The marbles may be black or white. Decide
how many marbles of each kind are in the jar. Shade the circles in the
jar to match your decision.

6. From 100 random draws you get:

a black marble ● 28 times

a white marble ○ 72 times

7. From 50 random draws you get:

a black marble ● 27 times

a white marble ○ 23 times

Use with Lesson 11.10.

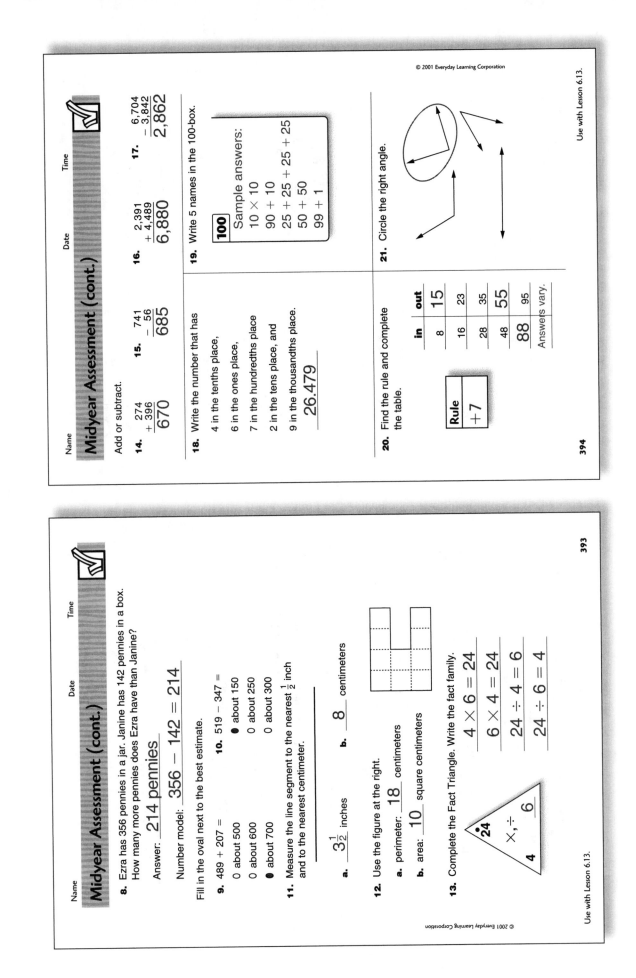

Name   Date   Time

Midyear Assessment (cont.)

8. Ezra has 356 pennies in a jar. Janine has 142 pennies in a box. How many more pennies does Ezra have than Janine?

Answer: __214__ pennies

Number model: __356 − 142 = 214__

Fill in the oval next to the best estimate.

9. 489 + 207 =
0 about 500
0 about 600
● about 700

10. 519 − 347 =
● about 150
0 about 250
0 about 300

11. Measure the line segment to the nearest $\frac{1}{2}$ inch and to the nearest centimeter.

a. __$3\frac{1}{2}$__ inches

b. __8__ centimeters

12. Use the figure at the right.

a. perimeter: __18__ centimeters

b. area: __10__ square centimeters

13. Complete the Fact Triangle. Write the fact family.

$4 \times 6 = 24$

$6 \times 4 = 24$

$24 \div 4 = 6$

$24 \div 6 = 4$

24
×, ÷
4   6

Use with Lesson 6.13.

393

Name   Date   Time

Midyear Assessment (cont.)

Add or subtract.

14.
```
  274
+ 396
-----
  670
```

15.
```
  741
-  56
-----
  685
```

16.
```
  2,391
+ 4,489
-------
  6,880
```

17.
```
  6,704
- 3,842
-------
  2,862
```

18. Write the number that has

4 in the tenths place,

6 in the ones place,

7 in the hundredths place

2 in the tens place, and

9 in the thousandths place.

__26.479__

19. Write 5 names in the 100-box.

100

Sample answers:

10×10

$90 + 10$

$25 + 25 + 25 + 25$

$50 + 50$

$99 + 1$

20. Find the rule and complete the table.

Rule
+7

in	out
8	15
16	23
28	35
48	55
88	95

Answers vary.

21. Circle the right angle.

Use with Lesson 6.13.

394

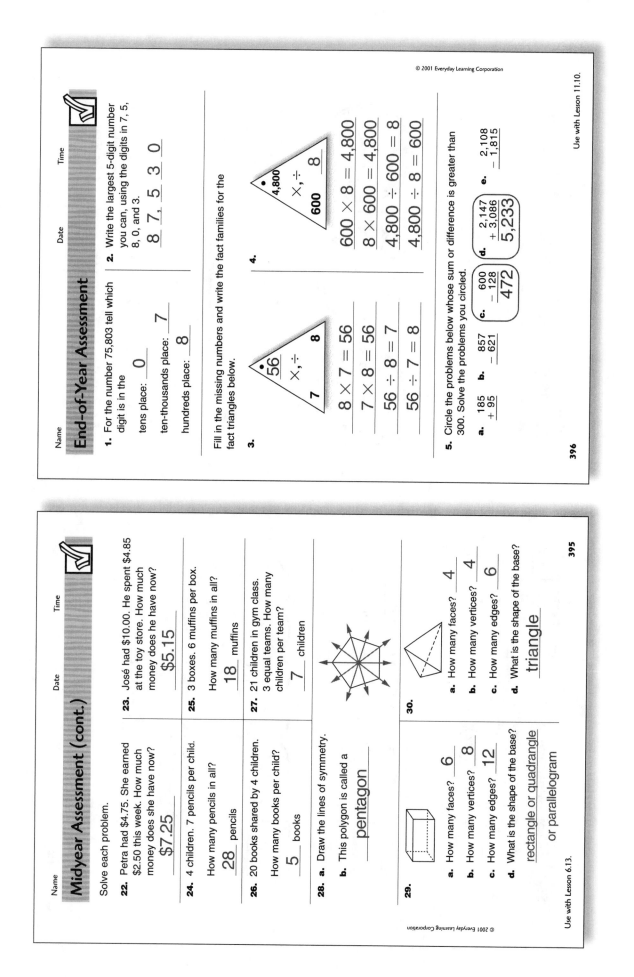

End-of-Year Assessment

Name ___ Date ___ Time ___

1. For the number 75,803 tell which digit is in the

   tens place: __0__

   ten-thousands place: __7__

   hundreds place: __8__

2. Write the largest 5-digit number you can, using the digits in 7, 5, 8, 0, and 3.

   8 7, 5 3 0

Fill in the missing numbers and write the fact families for the fact triangles below.

3.

56
×, ÷
7   8

8 × 7 = 56

7 × 8 = 56

56 ÷ 8 = 7

56 ÷ 7 = 8

4.

4,800
×, ÷
600   8

600 × 8 = 4,800

8 × 600 = 4,800

4,800 ÷ 600 = 8

4,800 ÷ 8 = 600

5. Circle the problems below whose sum or difference is greater than 300. Solve the problems you circled.

   a. 185
      + 95

   b.   857
       − 621

   c.   600
       − 128
       472

   d. 2,147
      + 3,086
       5,233

   e. 2,108
      − 1,815

Use with Lesson 11.10.

396

Midyear Assessment (cont.)

Name ___ Date ___ Time ___

Solve each problem.

22. Petra had $4.75. She earned $2.50 this week. How much money does she have now?

   $7.25

23. José had $10.00. He spent $4.85 at the toy store. How much money does he have now?

   $5.15

24. 4 children. 7 pencils per child. How many pencils in all?

   28 pencils

25. 3 boxes. 6 muffins per box. How many muffins in all?

   18 muffins

26. 20 books shared by 4 children. How many books per child?

   5 books

27. 21 children in gym class. 3 equal teams. How many children per team?

   7 children

28. a. Draw the lines of symmetry.

    b. This polygon is called a
       pentagon

29.
   a. How many faces? 6
   b. How many vertices? 8
   c. How many edges? 12
   d. What is the shape of the base?
      rectangle or quadrangle
      or parallelogram

30.
   a. How many faces? 4
   b. How many vertices? 4
   c. How many edges? 6
   d. What is the shape of the base?
      triangle

Use with Lesson 6.13.

395

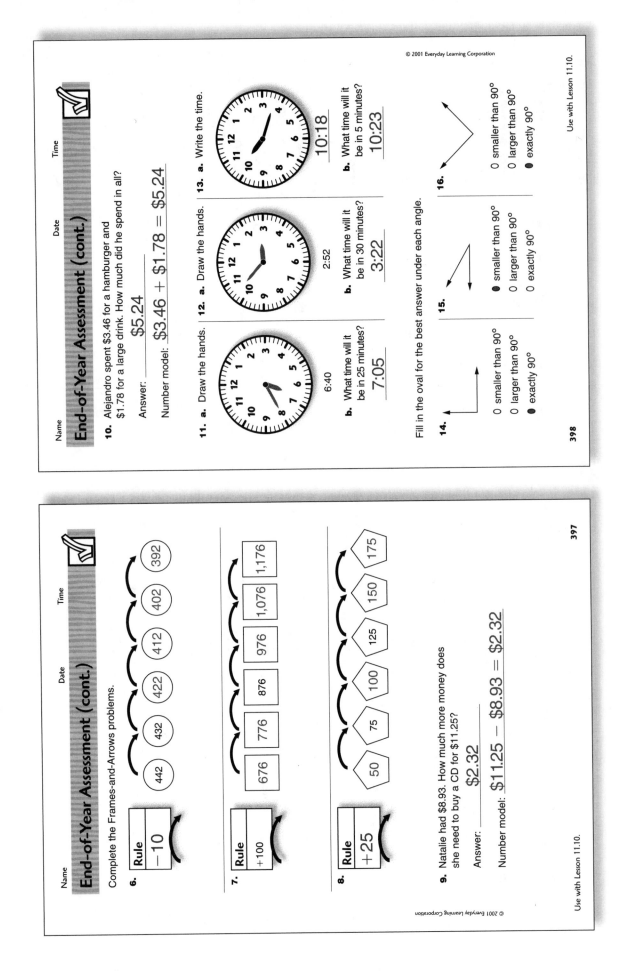

Name

Date

Time

End-of-Year Assessment (cont.)

Complete the Frames-and-Arrows problems.

6. Rule: −10

442 · 432 · 422 · 412 · 402 · 392

7. Rule: +100

676 · 776 · 876 · 976 · 1,076 · 1,176

8. Rule: +25

50 · 75 · 100 · 125 · 150 · 175

9. Natalie had $8.93. How much more money does she need to buy a CD for $11.25?

Answer: $2.32

Number model: $11.25 − $8.93 = $2.32

Use with Lesson 11.10.

397

Name

Date

Time

End-of-Year Assessment (cont.)

10. Alejandro spent $3.46 for a hamburger and $1.78 for a large drink. How much did he spend in all?

Answer: $5.24

Number model: $3.46 + $1.78 = $5.24

11. a. Draw the hands.

6:40

b. What time will it be in 25 minutes?

7:05

12. a. Draw the hands.

2:52

b. What time will it be in 30 minutes?

3:22

13. a. Write the time.

10:18

b. What time will it be in 5 minutes?

10:23

Fill in the oval for the best answer under each angle.

14.

O smaller than 90°
O larger than 90°
● exactly 90°

15.

● smaller than 90°
O larger than 90°
O exactly 90°

16.

O smaller than 90°
O larger than 90°
● exactly 90°

Use with Lesson 11.10.

398

Name _____ Date _____ Time _____

End-of-Year Assessment (cont.)

Fill in the oval for the name of each shape below.
(Part of the shape is hidden in Problem 20.)

17.
- ○ square
- ○ hexagon
- ● rhombus
- ○ trapezoid

18.
- ○ trapezoid
- ○ rhombus
- ○ octagon
- ● hexagon

19.
- ○ rhombus
- ● octagon
- ○ trapezoid
- ○ rectangle

20.
- ○ octagon
- ● trapezoid
- ○ rectangle
- ○ rhombus

21. Write another name for the shape in Problem 20 that is partly hidden. __quadrangle__

22. Find the perimeter and the area for the figure below.

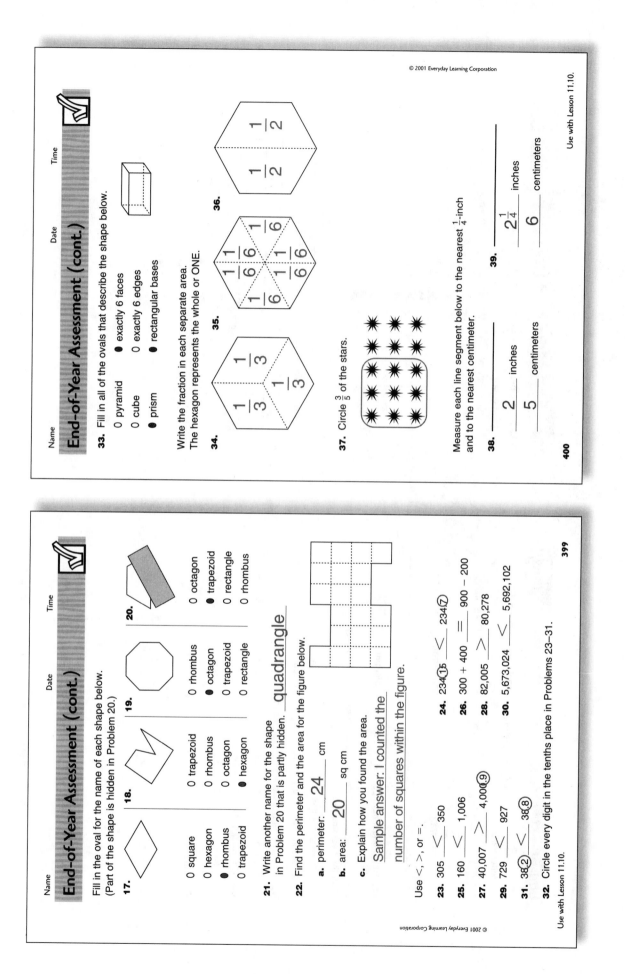

a. perimeter: __24__ cm

b. area: __20__ sq cm

c. Explain how you found the area.
Sample answer: I counted the number of squares within the figure.

Use <, >, or =.

23. 305 < 350

24. 234○15 < 234○7

25. 160 < 1,006

26. 300 + 400 = 900 − 200

27. 40,007 > 4,000○9

28. 82,005 > 80,278

29. 729 < 927

30. 5,673,024 < 5,692,102

31. 38○2 < 38○8

32. Circle every digit in the tenths place in Problems 23–31.

© 2001 Everyday Learning Corporation

Use with Lesson 11.10.

Name _____ Date _____ Time _____

End-of-Year Assessment (cont.)

© 2001 Everyday Learning Corporation

33. Fill in all of the ovals that describe the shape below.

- ○ pyramid   ● exactly 6 faces
- ○ cube   ○ exactly 6 edges
- ● prism   ● rectangular bases

Write the fraction in each separate area.
The hexagon represents the whole or ONE.

34. $\frac{1}{3}$ $\frac{1}{3}$ $\frac{1}{3}$ $\frac{1}{3}$

35. $\frac{1}{6}$ $\frac{1}{6}$ $\frac{1}{6}$ $\frac{1}{6}$ $\frac{1}{6}$ $\frac{1}{6}$

36. $\frac{1}{2}$ $\frac{1}{2}$

37. Circle $\frac{3}{5}$ of the stars.

Measure each line segment below to the nearest $\frac{1}{4}$-inch and to the nearest centimeter.

38. __2__ inches
__5__ centimeters

39. __$2\frac{1}{4}$__ inches
__6__ centimeters

Use with Lesson 11.10.

Name _____ Date _____ Time _____

End-of-Year Assessment (cont.)

40. On the top edge of the ruler below, label each mark with the letter listed.

$A: \frac{3}{4}$ in. $B: 4\frac{7}{8}$ in. $C: 1\frac{1}{4}$ in. $D: 1\frac{5}{8}$ in. $E: 2\frac{15}{16}$ in.

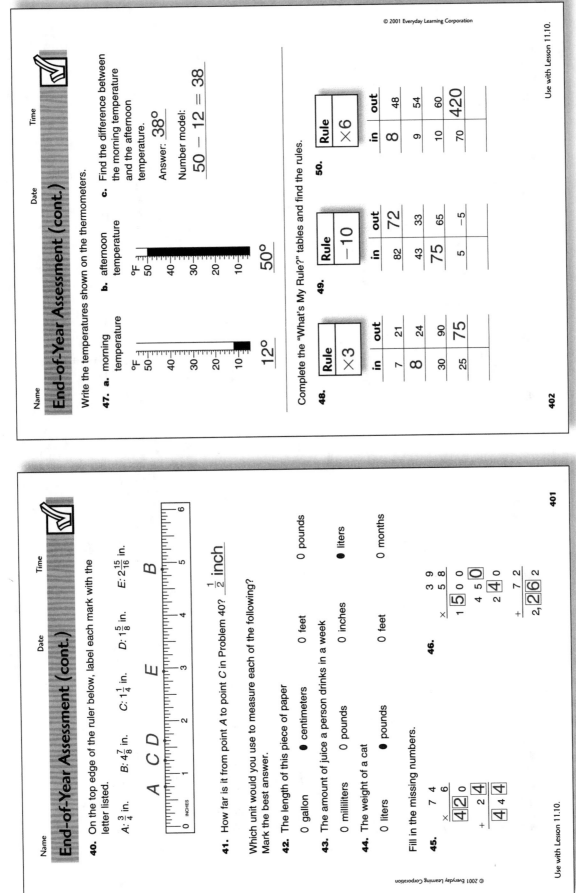

41. How far is it from point A to point C in Problem 40? $\frac{1}{2}$ inch

Which unit would you use to measure each of the following? Mark the best answer.

42. The length of this piece of paper
○ gallon ● centimeters ○ feet ○ pounds

43. The amount of juice a person drinks in a week
○ milliliters ○ pounds ○ inches ● liters

44. The weight of a cat
○ liters ● pounds ○ feet ○ months

Fill in the missing numbers.

45.
```
    7 4
  ×   6
  ─────
  4 2 0
+   2 4
  ─────
  4 4 4
```

46.
```
      3 9
    × 5 8
    ─────
  1 5 0 0
    4 5 0
    2 4 0
  +   7 2
  ───────
  2, 2 6 2
```

Name _____ Date _____ Time _____

End-of-Year Assessment (cont.)

Write the temperatures shown on the thermometers.

47. a. morning temperature **b.** afternoon temperature **c.** Find the difference between the morning temperature and the afternoon temperature.

12°   50°

Answer: 38°

Number model:
$$50 - 12 = 38$$

Complete the "What's My Rule?" tables and find the rules.

48.

Rule ×3	
in	**out**
7	21
8	24
30	90
25	75

49.

Rule −10	
in	**out**
82	72
43	33
75	65
5	−5

50.

Rule ×6	
in	**out**
8	48
9	54
10	60
70	420

Class Checklist: Unit 1

Class _____

Dates _____

Learning Goals

1a Identify and use number patterns to solve problems.
1b Count by 10s and 100s.
1c Apply place-value concepts in 4-digit numbers.
1d Tell and show times to the nearest minute.
1e Calculate the values of combinations of bills and coins and write the total using dollars-and-cents notation.
1f Find equivalent names for numbers.
1g Know addition facts.

Children's Names

1.
2.
3.
4.
5.
6.
7.
8.
9.
10.
11.
12.
13.
14.
15.
16.
17.
18.
19.
20.
21.
22.
23.
24.
25.
26.
27.
28.
29.
30.

Use with Lesson 1.13.

404

Name _____ Date _____ Time _____

End-of-Year Assessment (cont.)

51. Julia bought 4 boxes of pencils on sale.
There were 8 pencils in each box.
How many pencils did she buy altogether?

Answer: __32 pencils__

Number model: __$4 \times 8 = 32$__

52. Serita took a survey to see what kinds of pets her classmates had at home. Draw the graph to show her survey results and answer the questions.

Number of Children	Kind of Pet
5	Dog
6	Cat
4	Fish
1	Bird
5	Other

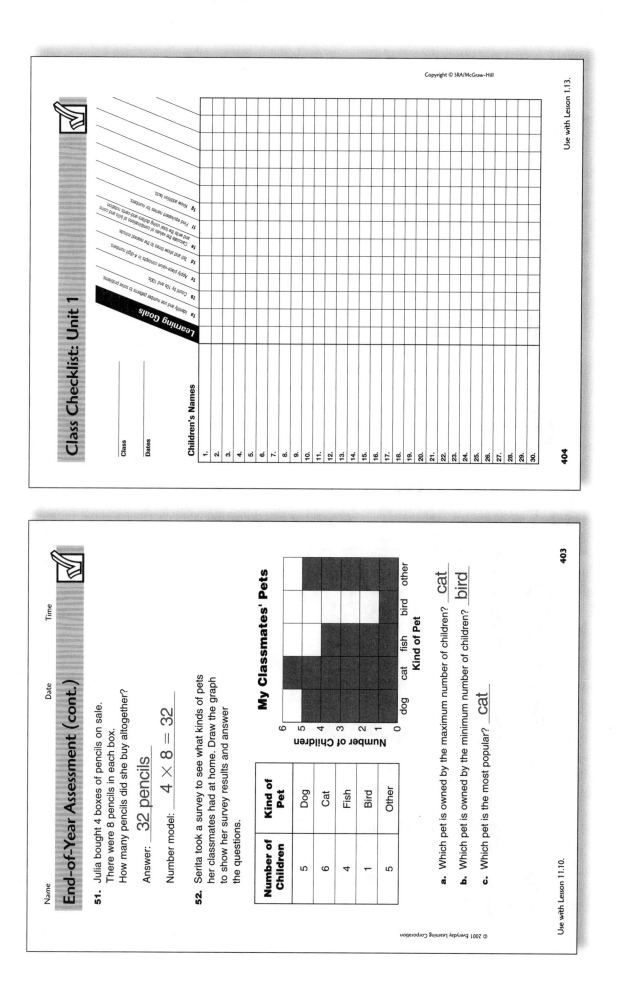

My Classmates' Pets

a. Which pet is owned by the maximum number of children? __cat__

b. Which pet is owned by the minimum number of children? __bird__

c. Which pet is the most popular? __cat__

Use with Lesson 11.10.

403

Class Checklist: Unit 2

Class _____

Dates _____

Learning Goals

2a Estimate answers to multidigit addition and subtraction problems.
2b Use basic facts to solve fact extensions.
2c Complete "What's My Rule?" tables.
2d Know addition and subtraction facts.
2e Complete fact and number families.
2f Solve addition and subtraction multidigit number stories.
2g Add multidigit numbers.
2h Subtract multidigit numbers.

Children's Names

1.
2.
3.
4.
5.
6.
7.
8.
9.
10.
11.
12.
13.
14.
15.
16.
17.
18.
19.
20.
21.
22.
23.
24.
25.
26.
27.
28.
29.
30.

406

Use with Lesson 2.10.

Child's Name _____   Date _____

Individual Profile of Progress: Unit 1

Check ✔			Learning Goals	Comments
B	D	S		
			1a Identify and use number patterns to solve problems.	
			1b Count by 10s and 100s.	
			1c Apply place-value concepts in 4-digit numbers.	
			1d Tell and show times to the nearest minute.	
			1e Calculate the values of combinations of bills and coins and write the total in dollars-and-cents notation.	
			1f Find equivalent names for numbers.	
			1g Know addition facts.	

Notes to Parents

_____

_____

_____

_____

_____

_____

B = Beginning; D = Developing; S = Secure

Use with Lesson 1.13.

405

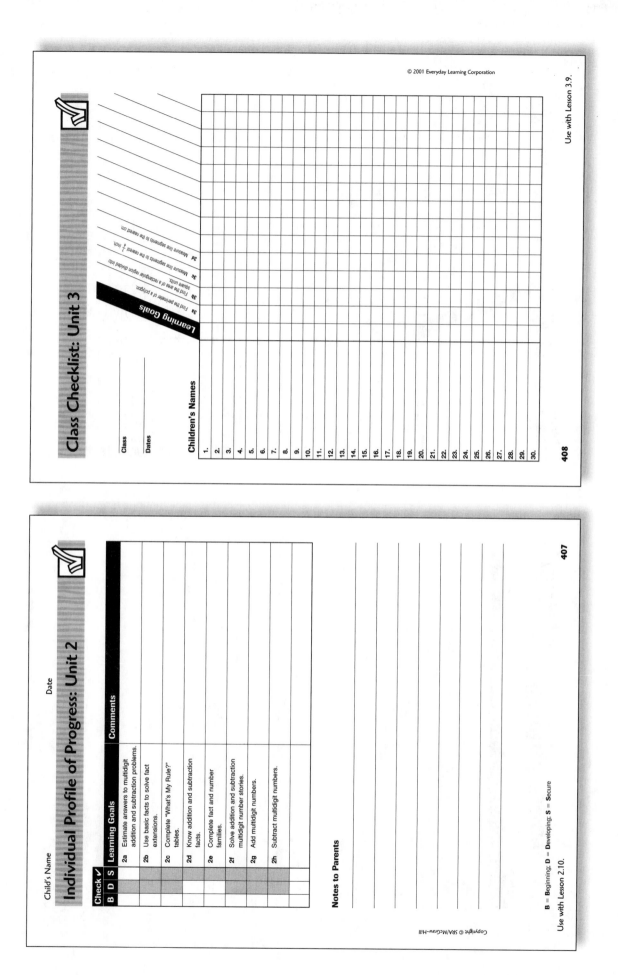

Class Checklist: Unit 3

Class _____

Dates _____

Learning Goals

- 3a Find the perimeter of a polygon.
- 3b Find the area of a rectangular region divided into square units.
- 3c Measure line segments to the nearest ½ inch.
- 3d Measure line segments to the nearest ¼ inch.
- 3e Measure line segments to the nearest cm.

Children's Names

1.
2.
3.
4.
5.
6.
7.
8.
9.
10.
11.
12.
13.
14.
15.
16.
17.
18.
19.
20.
21.
22.
23.
24.
25.
26.
27.
28.
29.
30.

© 2001 Everyday Learning Corporation

408

Use with Lesson 3.9.

Child's Name _____   Date _____

Individual Profile of Progress: Unit 2

Check			Learning Goals	Comments
B	**D**	**S**		
			2a Estimate answers to multidigit addition and subtraction problems.	
			2b Use basic facts to solve fact extensions.	
			2c Complete "What's My Rule?" tables.	
			2d Know addition and subtraction facts.	
			2e Complete fact and number families.	
			2f Solve addition and subtraction multidigit number stories.	
			2g Add multidigit numbers.	
			2h Subtract multidigit numbers.	

Notes to Parents

B = Beginning; **D** = Developing; **S** = Secure

Use with Lesson 2.10.

407

Class Checklist: Unit 4

Class _____

Dates _____

Learning Goals

4a Solve equal grouping number stories using multiplication.

4b Solve equal grouping and equal sharing number stories.

4c Know multiplication facts from the first set of fact triangles.

4d Know multiplication facts having the first set of fact factor.

4e Complete multiplication facts having 2, 5, or 10 as a factor.

4f Know multiplication/division fact families.

4g Know multiplication facts having 0 or 1 as a factor.

Children's Names

1.
2.
3.
4.
5.
6.
7.
8.
9.
10.
11.
12.
13.
14.
15.
16.
17.
18.
19.
20.
21.
22.
23.
24.
25.
26.
27.
28.
29.
30.

Use with Lesson 4.10.

410

Child's Name _____ Date _____

Individual Profile of Progress: Unit 3

Check ✔			Learning Goals	Comments
B	**D**	**S**		
			3a Find the perimeter of a polygon.	
			3b Find the area of a rectangular region divided into square units.	
			3c Measure line segments to the nearest $\frac{1}{4}$ inch.	
			3d Measure line segments to the nearest cm.	

Notes to Parents

B = Beginning; D = Developing; S = Secure

Use with Lesson 3.9.

409

Class Checklist: Unit 5

Class _____

Dates _____

Learning Goals

- **5a** Read, write, and compare 6- and 7-digit whole numbers.
- **5b** Read and write 3-digit decimals.
- **5c** Compare and order decimals.
- **5d** Identify place value in decimals.
- **5e** Read and write 1- and 2-digit decimals.
- **5f** Know multiplication facts from the first set of Fact Triangles.
- **5g** Read, write, and compare whole numbers up to 5 digits.
- **5h** Identify place value in whole numbers up to 5 digits.

Children's Names

1.
2.
3.
4.
5.
6.
7.
8.
9.
10.
11.
12.
13.
14.
15.
16.
17.
18.
19.
20.
21.
22.
23.
24.
25.
26.
27.
28.
29.
30.

Use with Lesson 5.13.

412

Child's Name _____   Date _____

Individual Profile of Progress: Unit 4

Check ✔

B	D	S		Learning Goals	Comments
			4a	Solve equal grouping number stories by using multiplication.	
			4b	Solve equal grouping and equal sharing number stories.	
			4c	Know multiplication facts from the first set of Fact Triangles.	
			4d	Know multiplication facts having 2, 5, or 10 as a factor.	
			4e	Complete multiplication/division fact families.	
			4f	Know multiplication facts having 0 or 1 as a factor.	

Notes to Parents

B = Beginning; **D** = Developing; **S** = Secure

Use with Lesson 4.10.

411

Class Checklist: Unit 6

Class _____

Dates _____

Learning Goals

6a Identify, draw, and name line segments, lines, and rays.

6b Draw parallel and intersecting line segments, lines, and rays.

6c Draw angles as records of rotations.

6d Know multiplication facts from the first set of Fact Triangles.

6e Identify right angles.

6f Identify and name 2-D and 3-D shapes.

6g Identify symmetric figures and draw lines of symmetry.

Children's Names

1.
2.
3.
4.
5.
6.
7.
8.
9.
10.
11.
12.
13.
14.
15.
16.
17.
18.
19.
20.
21.
22.
23.
24.
25.
26.
27.
28.
29.
30.

414

Use with Lesson 6.13.

Child's Name _____ Date _____

Individual Profile of Progress: Unit 5

Check ✓			Learning Goals	Comments
B	D	S		
			5a Read, write, and compare 6- and 7-digit whole numbers.	
			5b Read and write 3-digit decimals.	
			5c Compare and order decimals.	
			5d Identify place value in decimals.	
			5e Read and write 1- and 2-digit decimals.	
			5f Know multiplication facts from the first set of Fact Triangles.	
			5g Read, write, and compare whole numbers up to 5 digits.	
			5h Identify place value in whole numbers up to 5 digits.	

Notes to Parents

B = Beginning; D = Developing; S = Secure

Use with Lesson 5.13.

413

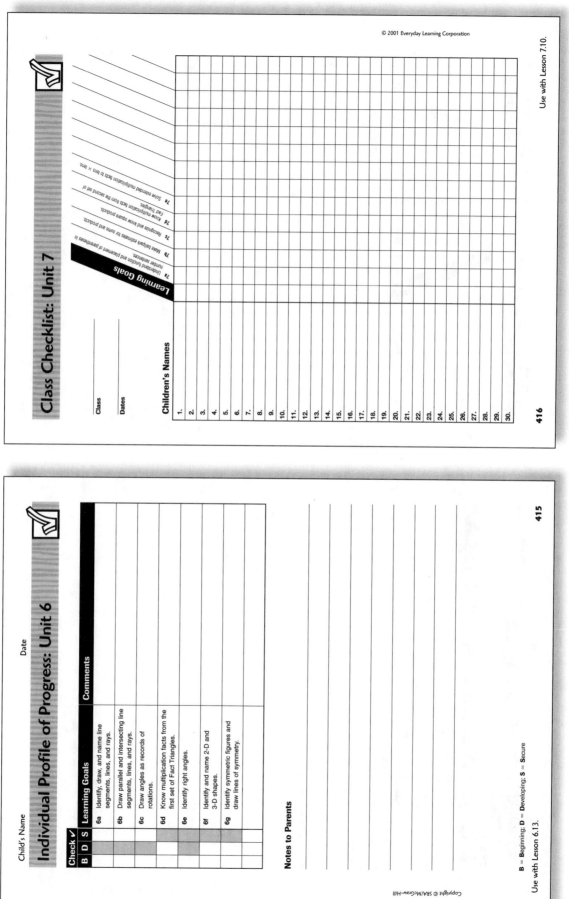

Class Checklist: Unit 7

Class _____

Dates _____

Learning Goals

7a Understand function and placement of parentheses in number sentences.

7b Make ballpark estimates for sums and products.

7c Recognize and know square products.

7d Know multiplication facts from the second set of Fact Triangles.

7e Solve extended multiplication facts to tens × tens.

Children's Names

1.
2.
3.
4.
5.
6.
7.
8.
9.
10.
11.
12.
13.
14.
15.
16.
17.
18.
19.
20.
21.
22.
23.
24.
25.
26.
27.
28.
29.
30.

© 2001 Everyday Learning Corporation

Use with Lesson 7.10.

416

Child's Name _____   Date _____

Individual Profile of Progress: Unit 6

Check ✓			Learning Goals	Comments
B	D	S		
			6a Identify, draw, and name line segments, lines, and rays.	
			6b Draw parallel and intersecting line segments, lines, and rays.	
			6c Draw angles as records of rotations.	
			6d Know multiplication facts from the first set of Fact Triangles.	
			6e Identify right angles.	
			6f Identify and name 2-D and 3-D shapes.	
			6g Identify symmetric figures and draw lines of symmetry.	

Notes to Parents

B = Beginning; D = Developing; S = Secure

Use with Lesson 6.13.

Copyright © SRA/McGraw-Hill

415

Class Checklist: Unit 8

Class _____

Dates _____

Learning Goals

- 8a Compare and order fractions.
- 8b Convert between mixed numbers and fractions.
- 8c Identify fractions on a number line.
- 8d Find equivalent fractions for given fractions.
- 8e Solve fraction number stories.
- 8f Identify fractional parts of a set.
- 8g Identify fractional parts of a region.

Children's Names

1.
2.
3.
4.
5.
6.
7.
8.
9.
10.
11.
12.
13.
14.
15.
16.
17.
18.
19.
20.
21.
22.
23.
24.
25.
26.
27.
28.
29.
30.

Use with Lesson 8.8.

418

Child's Name _____ Date _____

Individual Profile of Progress: Unit 7

Check ✔			Learning Goals	Comments
B	D	S		
			7a Understand function and placement of parentheses in number sentences.	
			7b Make ballpark estimates for sums and products.	
			7c Recognize and know square products.	
			7d Know multiplication facts from the second set of Fact Triangles.	
			7e Solve extended multiplication facts to tens × tens.	

Notes to Parents

B = Beginning; D = Developing; S = Secure

Use with Lesson 7.10.

417

Class Checklist: Unit 9

Class

Dates

Learning Goals

9a Solve number stories involving positive and negative integers.

9b Multiply multidigit numbers by 1- or 2-digit numbers.

9c Find factors of a number.

9d Interpret remainders in division problems.

9e Solve extended multiplication facts to hundreds times hundreds.

9f Solve equal grouping and equal sharing number stories.

Children's Names

1.
2.
3.
4.
5.
6.
7.
8.
9.
10.
11.
12.
13.
14.
15.
16.
17.
18.
19.
20.
21.
22.
23.
24.
25.
26.
27.
28.
29.
30.

420

Use with Lesson 9.14.

Child's Name _____ Date _____

Individual Profile of Progress: Unit 8

Check ✔			Learning Goals	Comments
B	D	S		
			8a Compare and order fractions.	
			8b Convert between mixed numbers and fractions.	
			8c Identify fractions on a number line.	
			8d Find equivalent fractions for given fractions.	
			8e Solve fraction number stories.	
			8f Identify fractional parts of a set.	
			8g Identify fractional parts of a region.	

Notes to Parents

B = **Beginning**; **D** = **Developing**; **S** = **Secure**

Use with Lesson 8.8.

419

Class Checklist: Unit 10

Class _____

Dates _____

Learning Goals

10a Find the volume of rectangular prisms.
10b Find the mean of a data set.
10c Find the median of a data set.
10d Measure to the nearest centimeter and inch.
10e Know units of measure for length, weight, and capacity.
10f Make a frequency table.
10g Know multiplication facts.
10h Make a bar graph.

Children's Names

1.
2.
3.
4.
5.
6.
7.
8.
9.
10.
11.
12.
13.
14.
15.
16.
17.
18.
19.
20.
21.
22.
23.
24.
25.
26.
27.
28.
29.
30.

Use with Lesson 10.12.

422

Child's Name _____   Date _____

Individual Profile of Progress: Unit 9

Check ✓			Learning Goals	Comments
B	D	S		
			9a Solve number stories involving positive and negative integers.	
			9b Multiply multidigit numbers by 1- or 2-digit numbers.	
			9c Find factors of a number.	
			9d Interpret remainders in division problems.	
			9e Solve extended multiplication facts to hundreds times hundreds.	
			9f Solve equal grouping and equal sharing number stories.	

Notes to Parents

B = Beginning; D = Developing; S = Secure

Use with Lesson 9.14.

421

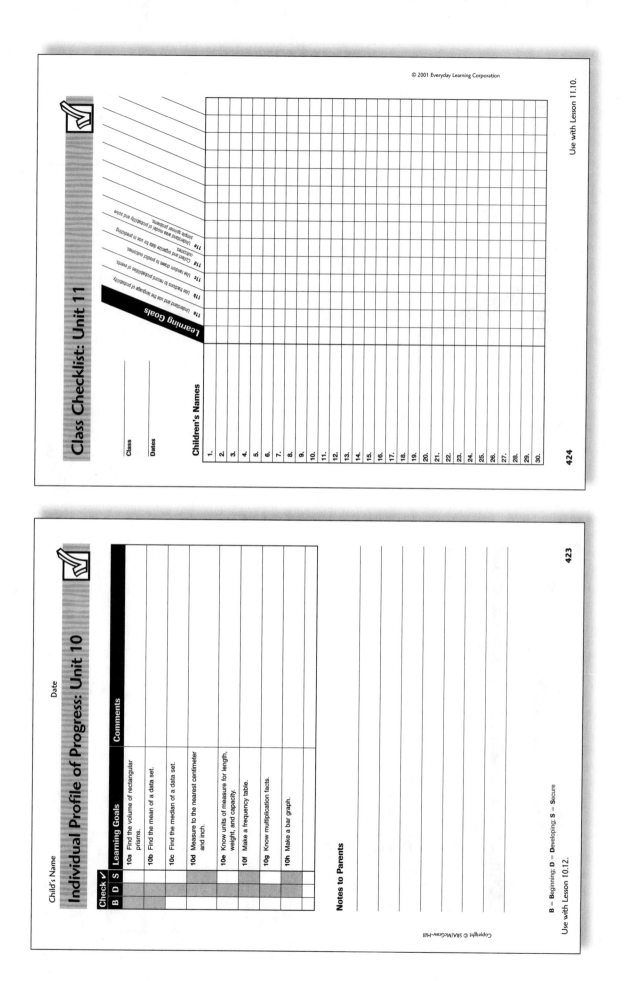

Class Checklist: Unit 11

Class _____

Dates _____

Learning Goals

- **11a** Understand and use the language of probability.
- **11b** Use fractions to record probabilities of events.
- **11c** Use random draws to predict outcomes.
- **11d** Collect and organize data for use in predicting outcomes.
- **11e** Understand area model of probability in predicting outcomes.
- **11f** Understand area model of probability and solve simple spinner problems.

Children's Names

1.
2.
3.
4.
5.
6.
7.
8.
9.
10.
11.
12.
13.
14.
15.
16.
17.
18.
19.
20.
21.
22.
23.
24.
25.
26.
27.
28.
29.
30.

Use with Lesson 11.10.

424

© 2001 Everyday Learning Corporation

Child's Name _____   Date _____

Individual Profile of Progress: Unit 10

Check ✔ B	D	S	Learning Goals	Comments
			10a Find the volume of rectangular prisms.	
			10b Find the mean of a data set.	
			10c Find the median of a data set.	
			10d Measure to the nearest centimeter and inch.	
			10e Know units of measure for length, weight, and capacity.	
			10f Make a frequency table.	
			10g Know multiplication facts.	
			10h Make a bar graph.	

Notes to Parents

B = Beginning; **D** = Developing; **S** = Secure

Use with Lesson 10.12.

423

Class Checklist: 1st Quarter

Class _____

Dates _____

Learning Goals

1. Identify and use number patterns to solve problems. (1a)
2. Count 10s and 100s. (1b)
3. Apply place-value concepts. (1c)
4. Calculate the values of combinations of bills and coins and write the total in dollars-and-cents notation. (1e)
5. Find equivalent names for numbers. (1f)
6. Tell and show times to the nearest minute. (1d)
7. Estimate answers to multidigit addition and subtraction problems. (2a)
8. Know addition and subtraction facts. (1g, 2d)
9. Complete fact and number families. (2e)
10. Add multidigit numbers. (2g)
11. Subtract multidigit numbers. (2h)
12. Complete "What's My Rule?" tables. (2s)

Children's Names

1.
2.
3.
4.
5.
6.
7.
8.
9.
10.
11.
12.
13.
14.
15.
16.
17.
18.
19.
20.
21.
22.
23.
24.
25.
26.
27.
28.
29.
30.

426 Use with Lesson 3.9.

Child's Name _____ Date _____

Individual Profile of Progress: Unit 11

Check ✔			Learning Goals	Comments
B	**D**	**S**		
			11a Understand and use the language of probability.	
			11b Use fractions to record probabilities of events.	
			11c Use random draws to predict outcomes.	
			11d Collect and organize data for use in predicting outcomes.	
			11e Understand area model of probability and solve simple spinner problems.	

Notes to Parents

B = Beginning; D = Developing; S = Secure

Use with Lesson 11.10.

425

Individual Profile of Progress: 1st Quarter

Child's Name _____ Date _____

Check ✓			Learning Goals	Comments
B	D	S		
			1. Identify and use number patterns to solve problems. (1a)	
			2. Count by 10s and 100s. (1b)	
			3. Apply place-value concepts in 4-digit numbers. (1c)	
			4. Calculate the values of combinations of bills and coins and write the total in dollars-and-cents notation. (1e)	
			5. Find equivalent names for numbers. (1f)	
			6. Tell and show times to the nearest minute. (1d)	
			7. Estimate answers to multidigit addition and subtraction problems. (2a)	
			8. Know addition and subtraction facts. (1g, 2d)	
			9. Complete fact and number families. (2e)	
			10. Add multidigit numbers. (2g)	
			11. Subtract multidigit numbers. (2h)	
			12. Complete "What's My Rule?" tables. (2c)	
			13. Use basic facts to solve fact extensions. (2b)	
			14. Solve addition and subtraction multidigit number stories. (2f)	
			15. Find the perimeter of a polygon. (3a)	
			16. Find the area of a rectangular region divided into square units. (3b)	
			17. Measure line segments to the nearest $\frac{1}{4}$ inch. (3c)	
			18. Measure line segments to the nearest cm. (3d)	

B = Beginning; **D** = Developing; **S** = Secure

428

Use with Lesson 3.9.

Class Checklist: 1st Quarter (cont.)

Class _____

Dates _____

Learning Goals

13.
14. Use basic facts to solve fact extensions. (2b)
15. Solve addition and subtraction multidigit number stories. (2f)
16. Find the perimeter of a polygon. (3a)
17. Find the area of a rectangular region divided into square units. (3b)
18. Measure line segments to the nearest $\frac{1}{4}$ inch. (3c)
19. Measure line segments to the nearest cm. (3d)

Children's Names

1.
2.
3.
4.
5.
6.
7.
8.
9.
10.
11.
12.
13.
14.
15.
16.
17.
18.
19.
20.
21.
22.
23.
24.
25.
26.
27.
28.
29.
30.

427

Use with Lesson 3.9.

Class Checklist: 2nd Quarter (cont.)

Class _____

Dates _____

Learning Goals

14. Read and write 3-digit decimals. **(5b)**
15. Identify, draw, and name line segments, lines, and rays. **(6a)**
16. Draw parallel and intersecting line segments, lines, and rays. **(6b)**
17. Draw angles as records of rotations. **(6c)**
18. Identify right angles. **(6e)**
19. Identify and name 2-D and 3-D shapes. **(6f)**
20. Identify symmetric figures and draw lines of symmetry. **(6g)**

Children's Names

1.
2.
3.
4.
5.
6.
7.
8.
9.
10.
11.
12.
13.
14.
15.
16.
17.
18.
19.
20.
21.
22.
23.
24.
25.
26.
27.
28.
29.
30.

430

Use with Lesson 6.13.

Class Checklist: 2nd Quarter

Class _____

Dates _____

Learning Goals

1. Solve equal grouping number stories by using multiplication. **(4a)**
2. Solve equal grouping and equal sharing number stories. **(4b)**
3. Know multiplication facts having 2, 5, or 10 as a factor. **(4d)**
4. Know multiplication facts having 0 or 1 as a factor. **(4f)**
5. Complete multiplication/division fact families. **(4e)**
6. Know multiplication facts from the first set of Fact Triangles. **(4c, 5f, 6d)**
7. Read, write, and compare whole numbers up to 5 digits. **(5g)**
8. Identify place value in whole numbers up to 5 digits. **(5h)**
9. Read, write, and compare 6- and 7-digit whole numbers. **(5a)**
10. Read and write 1- and 2-digit decimals. **(5e)**
11. Compare and order decimals. **(5c)**
12. Identify place value in decimals. **(5d)**

Children's Names

1.
2.
3.
4.
5.
6.
7.
8.
9.
10.
11.
12.
13.
14.
15.
16.
17.
18.
19.
20.
21.
22.
23.
24.
25.
26.
27.
28.
29.
30.

429

Use with Lesson 6.13.

Class Checklist: 3rd Quarter

Class _____

Dates _____

Learning Goals

1. Understand function and placement of parentheses in number sentences. **(7a)**
2. Make ballpark estimates for sums and products. **(7b)**
3. Recognize and know square products. **(7c)**
4. Know multiplication facts from the second set of Fact Triangles. **(7d)**
5. Solve extended multiplication facts to tens times tens. **(7e)**
6. Solve extended multiplication facts to tens times hundreds. **(7e)**
7. Multiply multidigit numbers by 1- or 2-digit numbers. **(9a)**
8. Find factors of a number. **(8c)**
9. Solve equal grouping and equal sharing number stories. **(9f)**
10. Interpret remainders in division problems. **(9d)**
11. Solve number stories involving positive and negative integers. **(9a)**
12. Compare and order fractions. **(8a)**

Children's Names

1.
2.
3.
4.
5.
6.
7.
8.
9.
10.
11.
12.
13.
14.
15.
16.
17.
18.
19.
20.
21.
22.
23.
24.
25.
26.
27.
28.
29.
30.

Use with Lesson 9.14.

432

Child's Name _____   Date _____

Individual Profile of Progress: 2nd Quarter

Check ✓			Learning Goals	Comments
B	D	S		
			1. Solve equal grouping number stories by using multiplication. **(4a)**	
			2. Solve equal grouping and equal sharing number stories. **(4b)**	
			3. Know multiplication facts having 2, 5, or 10 as a factor. **(4d)**	
			4. Complete multiplication/division fact families. **(4e)**	
			5. Know multiplication facts having 0 or 1 as a factor. **(4f)**	
			6. Know multiplication facts from the first set of Fact Triangles. **(4c, 5f, 6d)**	
			7. Read, write, and compare whole numbers up to 5 digits. **(5g)**	
			8. Identify place value in whole numbers up to 5 digits. **(5h)**	
			9. Read, write, and compare 6- and 7-digit whole numbers. **(5a)**	
			10. Read and write 1- and 2-digit decimals. **(5e)**	
			11. Compare and order decimals. **(5c)**	
			12. Identify place value in decimals. **(5d)**	
			13. Read and write 3-digit decimals. **(5b)**	
			14. Identify, draw, and name line segments, lines, and rays. **(6a)**	
			15. Draw parallel and intersecting line segments, lines, and rays. **(6b)**	
			16. Draw angles as records of rotations. **(6c)**	
			17. Identify right angles. **(6e)**	
			18. Identify and name 2-D and 3-D shapes. **(6f)**	
			19. Identify symmetric figures and draw lines of symmetry. **(6g)**	

B = **B**eginning; **D** = **D**eveloping; **S** = **S**ecure

Use with Lesson 6.13.

431

Individual Profile of Progress: 3rd Quarter

Child's Name _____ Date _____

Check ✓ B	D	S		Learning Goals	Comments
			1.	Understand function and placement of parentheses in number sentences. (7a)	
			2.	Make ballpark estimates for sums and products. (7b)	
			3.	Recognize and know square products. (7c)	
			4.	Know multiplication facts from the second set of Fact Triangles. (7d)	
			5.	Solve extended multiplication facts to tens times tens. (7e)	
			6.	Solve extended multiplication facts to hundreds times hundreds. (9e)	
			7.	Multiply multidigit numbers by 1- or 2-digit numbers. (9b)	
			8.	Find factors of a number. (9c)	
			9.	Solve equal grouping and equal sharing number stories. (9f)	
			10.	Interpret remainders in division problems. (9d)	
			11.	Solve number stories involving positive and negative integers. (9a)	
			12.	Compare and order fractions. (8a)	
			13.	Convert between mixed numbers and fractions. (8b)	
			14.	Identify fractions on a number line. (8c)	
			15.	Find equivalent fractions for given fractions. (8d)	
			16.	Solve fraction number stories. (8e)	
			17.	Identify fractional parts of a set. (8f)	
			18.	Identify fractional parts of a region. (8g)	

B = Beginning; D = Developing; S = Secure

434

Use with Lesson 9.14.

Class Checklist: 3rd Quarter (cont.)

Class _____

Dates _____

Children's Names

Learning Goals

12. Convert between mixed numbers and fractions. (8b)
14. Identify fractions on a number line. (8c)
15. Find equivalent fractions for given fractions. (8d)
16. Solve fraction number stories. (8e)
17. Identify fractional parts of a set. (8f)
18. Identify fractional parts of a region. (8g)

1. 2. 3. 4. 5. 6. 7. 8. 9. 10. 11. 12. 13. 14. 15. 16. 17. 18. 19. 20. 21. 22. 23. 24. 25. 26. 27. 28. 29. 30.

433

Use with Lesson 9.14.

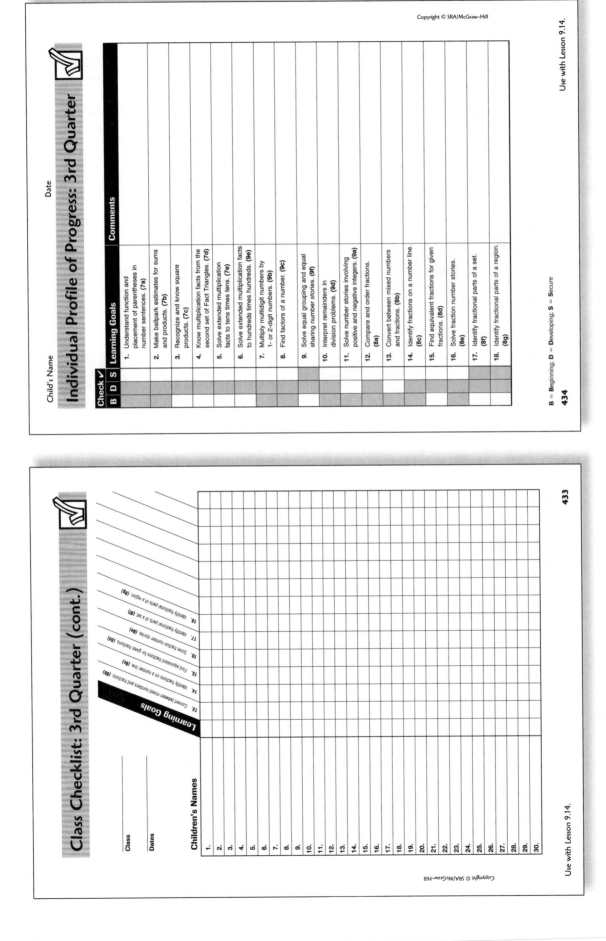

Individual Profile of Progress: 4th Quarter

Child's Name _____ Date _____

Check ✓			Learning Goals	Comments
B	D	S		
			1. Measure to the nearest centimeter and inch. (10d)	
			2. Know units of measure for length, weight, and capacity. (10e)	
			3. Find the volume of rectangular prisms. (10a)	
			4. Know multiplication facts. (10g)	
			5. Find the median of a data set. (10c)	
			6. Find the mean of a data set. (10b)	
			7. Make a bar graph. (10h)	
			8. Make a frequency table. (10f)	
			9. Understand and use the language of probability. (11a)	
			10. Use fractions to record probabilities of events. (11b)	
			11. Use random draws to predict outcomes. (11c)	
			12. Collect and organize data for use in predicting outcomes. (11d)	
			13. Understand area model of probability and solve simple spinner problems. (11e)	

Notes to Parents

_____

_____

_____

436

Use with Lesson 11.10.

Class Checklist: 4th Quarter

Class _____

Dates _____

Learning Goals

1. Measure to the nearest centimeter and inch. (10d)
2. Know units of measure for length, weight, and capacity. (10e)
3. Find the volume of rectangular prisms. (10a)
4. Know multiplication facts. (10g)
5. Find the median of a data set. (10c)
6. Find the mean of a data set. (10b)
7. Make a bar graph. (10h)
8. Make a frequency table. (10f)
9. Understand and use the language of probability. (11a)
10. Use fractions to record probabilities of events. (11b)
11. Use random draws to predict outcomes. (11c)
12. Collect and organize data for use in predicting outcomes. (11d)
13. Understand area model of probability and solve simple spinner problems. (11e)

Children's Names

1.
2.
3.
4.
5.
6.
7.
8.
9.
10.
11.
12.
13.
14.
15.
16.
17.
18.
19.
20.
21.
22.
23.
24.
25.
26.
27.
28.
29.
30.

435

Use with Lesson 11.10.

List of Assessment Sources

Ongoing Assessment

Product Assessment

Periodic Assessment

Outside Tests

Other

Use as needed.

437

Child's Name _____ Date _____

Individual Profile of Progress

Check ✔			Learning Goals	Comments
B	D	S		
			1.	
			2.	
			3.	
			4.	
			5.	
			6.	
			7.	
			8.	
			9.	
			10.	

Notes to Parents

B = Beginning; **D** = Developing; **S** = Secure

Use as needed.

438

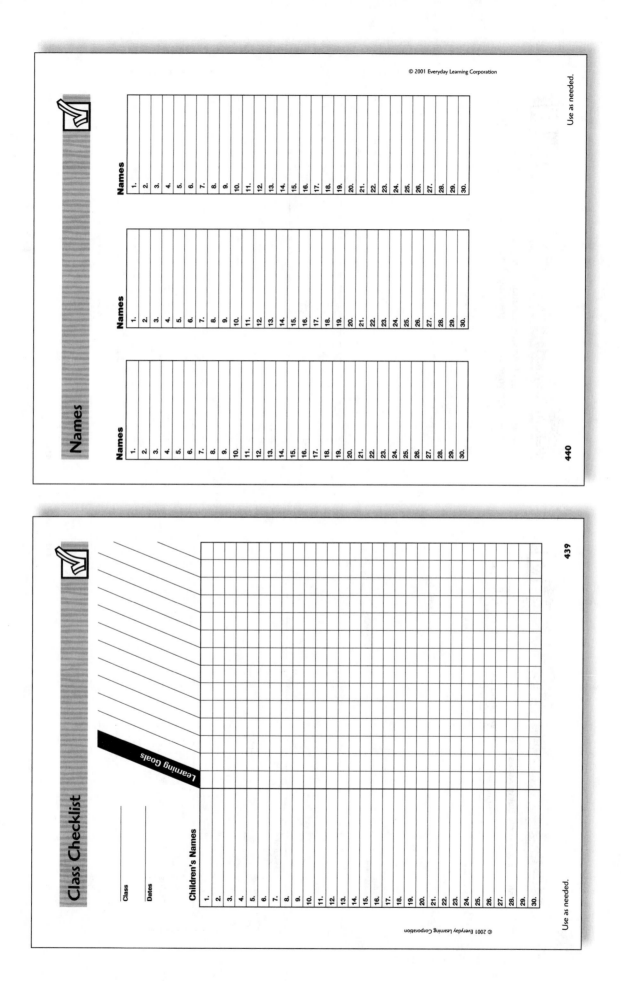

Names

Names

1.
2.
3.
4.
5.
6.
7.
8.
9.
10.
11.
12.
13.
14.
15.
16.
17.
18.
19.
20.
21.
22.
23.
24.
25.
26.
27.
28.
29.
30.

Names

1.
2.
3.
4.
5.
6.
7.
8.
9.
10.
11.
12.
13.
14.
15.
16.
17.
18.
19.
20.
21.
22.
23.
24.
25.
26.
27.
28.
29.
30.

Names

1.
2.
3.
4.
5.
6.
7.
8.
9.
10.
11.
12.
13.
14.
15.
16.
17.
18.
19.
20.
21.
22.
23.
24.
25.
26.
27.
28.
29.
30.

Use as needed.

440

Class Checklist

Class _____

Dates _____

Learning Goals

Children's Names

1.
2.
3.
4.
5.
6.
7.
8.
9.
10.
11.
12.
13.
14.
15.
16.
17.
18.
19.
20.
21.
22.
23.
24.
25.
26.
27.
28.
29.
30.

Use as needed.

439

Parent Reflections

Child's Name _____ Date _____

Use some of the following questions (or your own) and tell us how you see your child progressing in mathematics:

Do you see evidence of your child using mathematics at home?

What do you think are your child's strengths and challenges in mathematics?

Does your child demonstrate responsibility for completing Home Links?

What thoughts do you have about your child's progress in mathematics?

Use as needed.

442

Class Progress Indicator

Mathematical Topic Being Assessed: _____

	BEGINNING	DEVELOPING OR DEVELOPING+	SECURE OR SECURE+
First Assessment After Lesson: _____ Dates included: _____ to _____			
Second Assessment After Lesson: _____ Dates included: _____ to _____			
Third Assessment After Lesson: _____ Dates included: _____ to _____			

Notes

Use as needed.

441

About My Math Class

© 2001 Everyday Learning Corporation

Name _____   Date _____   Time _____

Draw a face or write the words that show how you feel.

Good   OK   Not so good

1. This is how I feel about math:	**2.** This is how I feel about working with a partner or in a small group:	**3.** This is how I feel about working by myself:
4. This is how I feel about solving number stories:	**5.** This is how I feel about doing Home Links with my family:	**6.** This is how I feel about finding new ways to solve problems

Circle **yes, sometimes,** or **no.**

7. I like to figure things out. I am curious.

    yes   **sometimes**   **no**

8. I keep trying even when I don't understand something right away.

    yes   **sometimes**   **no**

Use as needed.

444

Rubric

Beginning (B)

Developing (D)

Secure (S)

© 2001 Everyday Learning Corporation

Use as needed.

443

Math Log A

Name _____ Date _____ Time _____

What did you learn in mathematics this week?

_____
_____
_____
_____
_____
_____
_____
_____

Use as needed.

446

About My Math Class

Name _____ Date _____ Time _____

Circle the word that best describes how you feel.

1. I enjoy mathematics class.   **yes**   **sometimes**   **no**

2. I like to work with a partner
   or in a group.   **yes**   **sometimes**   **no**

3. I like to work by myself.   **yes**   **sometimes**   **no**

4. I like to solve problems
   in mathematics.   **yes**   **sometimes**   **no**

5. I enjoy doing Home Links
   with my family.   **yes**   **sometimes**   **no**

6. In mathematics, I am good at _____
   _____

7. One thing I like about mathematics is _____
   _____

8. One thing I find difficult in mathematics is _____
   _____

Use as needed.

445

Name _____ Date _____ Time _____

Math Log C

Work Box

Tell how you solved
this problem.

_____

_____

_____

_____

Use as needed.

448

Name _____ Date _____ Time _____

Math Log C

Work Box

Tell how you solved
this problem.

_____

_____

_____

_____

Use as needed.

448

Name _____ Date _____ Time _____

Math Log B

Question: _____

_____

_____

_____

_____

_____

_____

_____

_____

Use as needed.

447

Assessment Masters

My Work

Name

Date

Time

This work shows that I can _____

_____

_____

_____

I am still learning to _____

_____

_____

Use as needed.

450

My Work

Name

Date

Time

This is what I know about _____

_____

_____

_____

_____

_____

Use as needed.

450

Good Work!

Name

Date

Time

:) I like this work because _____

_____

_____

_____

_____

_____

_____

_____

_____

_____

_____

Use as needed.

449

Name _____ Date _____ Time _____

Name Collections

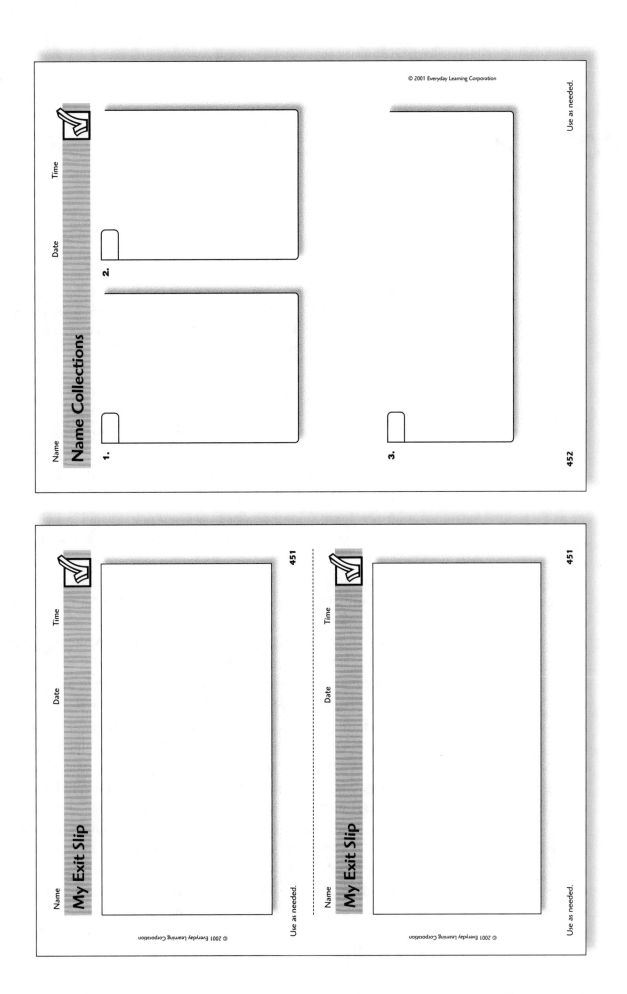

1.

2.

3.

452

Use as needed.

Name _____ Date _____ Time _____

My Exit Slip

451

Use as needed.

Name _____ Date _____ Time _____

My Exit Slip

451

Use as needed.

Glossary

assessment The gathering of information about children's progress. This information might include children's knowledge and use of mathematics, as well as their feelings about mathematics. The assessment is used to draw conclusions for individual and class instruction.

assessment sources Mathematical tasks or interactions that can be used for gathering data for assessment purposes.

concepts Basic mathematical ideas that are fundamental in guiding reasoning and problem solving in unfamiliar situations.

evaluation Judgments based on information gathered during assessment.

interviews Conversations between a teacher and individual children during which the teacher can obtain information useful for assessing mathematical progress.

kid-watching The observing and recording of children's interactions and communications during regular instructional activities.

long-term projects Mathematical activities that may require days, weeks, or months to complete.

Mathematics Interest Inventories A written format for assessing children's attitudes toward mathematics.

Math Logs Formats for developing written communication while gathering examples of children's mathematical thinking through writing, pictures, diagrams, and so on.

Ongoing Assessment The gathering of assessment data during regular instructional activities.

open-ended questions Questions that have multiple answers and ways of arriving at these answers. (Open-ended questions are good assessments for problem-solving and reasoning skills.)

outside tests School, district, state, or standardized tests. These tests may or may not match the curriculum.

performance The carrying out or completing of a mathematical activity that displays children's knowledge and judgment while they are engaged in the activity.

Periodic Assessment The more formal gathering of assessment information, often outside of regular instructional time. One example is end-of-unit assessment.

portfolio A sample collection of a child's mathematical work representing his or her progress over the school year.

Product Assessment Samples of children's work, including pictures, diagrams, or concrete representations.

progress The growth, development, and continuous improvement of children's mathematical abilities.

Progress Indicators A form upon which the results of sequential assessment tasks for various mathematical ideas, routines, and concepts can be recorded for the whole class during the school year, using such indicator categories as Beginning, Developing, and Secure.

reflective writing The ability to reflect and write about mathematics, on topics like accomplishments, confidence, feelings, understanding or lack of understanding, goals, and so on.

representative work A piece of work that represents a child's ability and that indicates progress made.

rubric A defined set of guidelines that gives direction for scoring assessment activities. The most useful rubrics are those derived from experience with a wide variety of performances of an assessment task.

self-assessment The ability of children to judge, reflect on, and acknowledge the quality of their mathematical thinking or productions.

standardized tests Typically, nationwide tests that are given, scored, and interpreted in a very consistent way, regardless of the population being tested.

validity of assessment The degree to which assessment data actually represent the knowledge, thought processes, and skills that children have attained.

Index